More Praise for *The Winning Family:*

"An inspiring book that can improve the quality of family life."
—Library Journal

"Practical and insightful. A super book!"
—Dr. Christopher Green, pediatrician,
author of *Toddler Taming*

"Never has a book been so meaningful and timely! It has all the essentials: theory, practicality, application, and passion for kids. Self-esteem *must* start with the family. And *The Winning Family* needs to be in every home."
—Dr. Michele Borba, author, *Esteem Builders*
and *Self-Esteem: A Classroom Affair*

"This book is a must for parents who want to raise healthy children."
—Patricia G. Palmer Ed.D.,
Clinical psychologist and author

"A wonderfully readable and understandable presentation of the best insights into better parenting."
—Peter D. Lenn Ph.D., Founder and President
of Active Learning, Inc.

"Great book! An excellent primer for every parent."
—Andy Mecca, Chairperson, California Task
Force to Promote Self-Esteem and Personal
and Social Responsibility

"At last there is a book that goes beyond parenting to focusing on the personal development of parents along with the development of their children."
—Jeanne Gibbs, author of *Tribes*

"This book covers in a very insightful way all of the major stumbling blocks which lead to major dysfunctions in nuclear families. Positive. Hopeful."
—Constance A. Jones, Associate Professor of
Sociology, Mills College

"Packed with helpful insights and suggestions."
—Jean Illsley Clarke, Author of
Self-Esteem: A Family Affair

"Exceptional in content and style. Outstanding readability. The number one book I recommend to families. It's changed so many lives."
—Nevin Saunders, Parent Educator
California Parenting Institute

"This book has become our second Bible."
—Linda Schuler, mother and student, Illinois

"As a former family day care provider, I wish I had had this book 21 years ago when I first became a parent! This is 'must reading' for all care givers of children. I read it cover to cover in one day."
—Sandra Gellert, National Association for Family Day Care

"I use this book all the time in counseling suicidal teenagers."
—Don Burchfield, Counselor Phoenix, Arizona

"I am a recovering alcoholic and it's helped me very much. My self-esteem has really gone up and so has my boys'. Our lives are an adventure today. We are able to love each other like never before."
—Name withheld, Florida

"Every page is an invitation and a challenge to put every word into action. The insights will help bridge the gap between me and my son."
—Bob Hill, father, New York

"So much harm is done in the name of 'love'. The more people who can hear your message, the better our world will be."
—Kathy Seymour, New York

"I am an Adult Child of an Alcoholic and have been in group therapy for some time. This book covers so many of the topics that are involved in therapy."
—Nancy Gants, Ohio

"This is the only book I took to the hospital when I delivered my baby. It's dynamic!"
—Laurel Hameon, New South Wales, Australia

"The best book I have read in years. It captured my interest from beginning to end. I'm a single mother raising a boy diagnosed with neurological problems. I was 'losing it.' Reading a bit of this book every day put a lot of things into perspective for me and helped me in this difficult time."
—Name withheld, New Jersey

"I am a mother of four children who is currently going through a divorce. *The Winning Family* is what I need to help with the rebuilding of my family."
—Name withheld, Kentucky

The Winning Family

Increasing Self-Esteem
in Your Children
and Yourself

The Winning Family

Increasing Self-Esteem in Your Children and Yourself

Dr. Louise Hart

Illustrated by
Kristen Baumgardner

Published by LifeSkills Press,
P. O. Box 9276, Oakland, CA 94613
Manufactured in the United States of America
Printed on recycled paper.

Book design by Suzanne Babeuf
Cover design by Richard Rossiter

New Revised Edition

2 3 4 5 6 7 8 9 10

Library of Congress Cataloging-in-Publication Data

Hart, Louise.

The winning family.

Bibliography:p.
Includes index.
1. Self-respect. 2. Self-respect in children.
3. Child rearing. I. Title.
89-80900

ISBN O-9622834-1-X

Choose the way of life.
Choose the way of love.
Choose the way of caring.
Choose the way of hope.
Choose the way of belief in tomorrow.
Choose the way of trusting.
Choose the way of goodness.
It's up to you. It's your choice.
—Leo F. Buscaglia[1]

Contents

Acknowledgements
Introduction

1. You Are Building a Cathedral   1
2. The Greatest Gift: Self-Esteem   5
3. Self-Esteem Protection Skills   13
4. "I Know They Love Me, But I Don't Feel It."   17
5. Listening Skills   21
6. Asking and Refusal Skills   25
7. Dealing With Feelings   29
8. The Power of Words   43
9. Parenting Responses That Affect Self-Esteem   51
10. Parents Are Leaders: Re-Visioning Your Family   57
11. Parenting Leadership Styles   63
12. Parenting and Empowerment   71
13. For Your Own Good: Discipline Without Damage   79
14. Guidance   89
15. Problem Solving   93
16. Touch   101
17. Beliefs   109
18. Self-Talk   113
19. Obsession With Perfectionism   121

20. Cultural Barriers to Self-Esteem   127
21. Who's Pulling Your Strings?   145
22. Play   149
23. The Winning Environment   155
24. Extending Your Family   157
25. The Winning Family   161

Postscript: On Nightmares   165
Appendices   169
Resources Available to Parents   175
Recommended Reading   177
Notes   179
Index   185

Acknowledgements

This book is dedicated to my children, Damian, Kristen, and Felix Baumgardner with gratitude and love. They have been my best cheerleaders. It is also dedicated to the many parents who have shared their struggles, successes and insights; and to my friend, Kathy May, who believed in me before I believed in myself.

My special thanks to Kate Fotopoulos, editor of the first edition, and my daughter, Kristen Baumgardner, editor of the revised edition. I appreciate their dependability and skill in helping me put onto paper the concepts that are closest to my heart.

Introduction

I have written for you the book I wish had been available to me twenty years ago—and to my mother forty years ago, and to her mother before that. But we cannot turn back time. We must begin where we are now and move forward.

The biological parent-child connection is the deepest natural bond. It continues even after separation by death. From the moment they first appear, children introduce a totally new dimension into our lives that expands, challenges, deepens, sweetens, and at times exhausts us. Our children present us with ongoing opportunities to grow.

I write as a parent who has been there—stretching and growing in the process of my own life—and also as a community psychologist trying to prevent mental illness through teaching lifeskills for building healthier, happier individuals and families.

Like many people today, I have lived in a variety of family forms. When I was born, my mother ran the household while my father worked outside the home. I had the benefit of living in an extended family and had relatives other than my parents to look to as models. After college I got married, taught school for four years, and then was a full-time, stay-at-home mom in my nuclear family for thirteen years.

During that time my young family moved to Colorado. My mother, brothers, and sister lived a thousand miles east and west, so the family had little contact with grandparents, aunts, uncles, and cousins. We were relatively isolated until my husband's parents moved west and settled about thirty miles away from us.

At the time of this writing, my family has yet another form. After living for several years in a single-parent household, my three children are now attending college, working, and discovering the world, while my lectures and workshops are taking me around the country and beyond. Living separately, we look forward with excitement to our reunions.

Families come in many diverse forms and sizes, from large extended families to a "family of one;" the specifics change over the course of a lifetime. Regardless of the living arrangements, deep connections will always link family members. This book can be helpful for any person, from any type of family, who wants to let go of dysfunctional patterns and reach for health, joy, and satisfaction—who believes that everyone can be a winner and no one has to lose. The information is also relevant to special populations, to child care providers, and to educators. It is helpful to anyone who works with or cares for children—or has been a child.

A Winning Family begins with good intentions. Yet good intentions are not enough. We must re-examine what we know about raising children. *We need to learn from old mistakes rather than repeat them.* We need to be willing to examine and replace negative habits and patterns in our own lives. Raising our children differently can help us heal our past.

Since we can't give what we don't have, we need to learn how to raise our own self-esteem along with our children's. Self-esteem is the greatest gift a parent can give to a child—certainly the most important! Parents can lay a solid, loving foundation early in the lives of their children that builds self-esteem before the outside world has a major impact. *An ounce of prevention is worth a pound of cure.*

Parents can help *prevent low self-esteem*—and keep their loved ones from:

- vulnerability to negative peer pressure
- drug and alcohol and other abuses
- teen pregnancy
- dropping out of school
- eating disorders
- other addictive behaviors
- crime and violence
- suicide

And parents can *promote high self-esteem* so that their children:

- resist dependencies and addictions
- are enthusiastic about life (and school!)
- make friends easily
- trust themselves
- are self-directed
- are cooperative and follow reasonable rules
- are creative and imaginative
- take pride in their achievements
- are basically happy individuals
- are an asset to society and to the world!

With three children of my own, I have come to learn that parents have a great deal of influence and control over children's lives; we have control over family rules, communication styles, and family climate. Of course, there are areas in which we have little or no control. The cultural climate profoundly affects us all; we are cast into its mold. Yet at the same time, we also create it. Seen in this light, culture can limit or expand us, entrap or enhance us. If we clearly identify dangers, we can empower our children to cope with problems and challenges, to make choices instead of being victims.

The Winning Family delves into commonly encountered problems and offers healthy solutions. It teaches new skills to effectively meet the challenges of living with and raising kids in a complex world.

There is no one right way to parent, there are many. And you need to find the way that works for you. Become an expert on your family— you know them better than anyone else. Learn to trust yourself. Learn to take good care of yourself, for your own sake and for theirs.

There is not just one right way to use this book. I encourage you to read a bit, try out some of the techniques described, then go back and read some more. It doesn't matter how long it takes you to get through the book. Your reward will come from putting it into practice.

Parenting can be a loving and enjoyable experience. If it's not, look for new skills, new methods, and new strategies that will be effective in your situation. And as a tennis pro once said, "If your game's not working, change it."

I support you and believe in you. And I thank you for working to shape a better world for our children.

Louise Hart

1.

You Are Building a Cathedral

*"Our children give us the opportunity to become the parents
we always wished we'd had."*

—L. Hart[1]

Many years ago, two men were working at the same job on the out-
skirts of a European city. A stranger approached them and asked,
"What are you doing?" The first man replied with an edge of resentment, "I'm hauling rocks." The second man, when asked the same
question, enthusiastically replied, "I'm building a cathedral!"

Just as skilled craftsmen designed cathedrals to be inspiring, to
stand tall and strong, and to resist the elements over the years, we
who raise and teach and care for children are working to build in
them the strength and skills to live happy, creative, productive lives.
This vitally important work is too often unsupported and under-
valued.

We are the products of our families, our culture, and our time—
and of these three, family has the strongest influence. My parents
gave me more than they ever received. As children, they had had
difficult times in Germany. The first of twelve children, my mother
grew up with adult responsibilities. Her mother had died delivering
the fourth baby, and her father's new wife continued to have and
raise children.

The primary focus in that family was survival; the primary value
was work. And my parents transmitted those values to us. With the
best of intentions, they did all they could for their children. But
they couldn't give what they didn't have. "How can I love when I
never was loved?" my mother once asked.

Many people operate under the assumption that since parenting
is a natural function of adult human beings, we should instinctively
know how to do it—and do it well. The truth is, effective parenting
requires study and practice like any other skilled profession. Who

would even consider turning an untrained surgeon loose in an operating room? Yet we "operate" on our children every day.

Things just weren't right for me as a child. I was confused, lost, and lonely. I felt unloved. I had no self-esteem—I had no sense of self. When I was pregnant with my first child in the early 1960's, I made a very important decision—probably the most important decision of my life. I made a commitment: to raise my children the way I would like to have been raised. This was not easy to do since I had no models. I became (as did other parents around me) a pioneer. After examining and reexamining everything I knew about parenting, I gave my kids what I thought was best.

My children, now young adults, are basically healthy, happy, responsible individuals with good self-esteem. What continues to delight me is that I receive from them what I have given: acceptance, respect, love, and support. Children deserve the best, and *over time what goes around, comes around.*

As children, we had no choice about how we were parented. As parents, we have the choice to teach *unconsciously* by repeating the patterns used with us—or we can *make a conscious commitment* to passing on only those values we would like to see perpetuated.

For better or worse, you probably learned how to parent from your parents. You were taught by the examples they set: what they were is what you learned. If you felt loved and valued as a child and if you've become a competent, healthy adult, you were fortunate to have had good modeling. Thank your parents. Raising kids should be relatively easy for you. But if you do not like the way you were raised—if you were rejected, neglected, or abused in any way, if you grew up in an alcoholic or other dysfunctional family system—you can choose differently. *You can rise above old, destructive patterns* to create a healthy life for yourself and your family.

A good place to start is by taking an honest look at your own childhood. Remember what it was like growing up in your family. What did your parents do to make you feel loved? How did they discipline you? How did they communicate and resolve problems with you and each other? What helped you to feel good about yourself, and what led you to conclude that you were "bad", that there was something wrong with you? Try not to idealize your experiences. Glossing over painful memories leaves you at greater risk of repeating those behaviors with your own children.

We learned to parent from our mothers and fathers. Being human, they made mistakes. *We can choose to learn from those mistakes rather than passing them on. We can choose to heal ourselves rather than wounding our children.*

In order to become conscious parents, we need to question, sift, and sort through old "tapes," habits, and patterns. *Pass on the best— and throw away the rest.* This commitment is our best assurance that whatever negative patterns we may have grown up with will not be repeated in our children's generation.

We live in an exciting time. More and more parents are becoming conscious of how they are parenting rather than unconsciously doing to their children what was done to them. Today we are becoming more and more aware of the impact our choices have on our children's future. *With awareness comes choice.* We can choose to look back at our childhoods, identify the consequences of various parenting strategies, and sort them into "growthful" or "harmful." Then we can consciously pick the ones we want to hand down to our own children.

Both negative and positive experiences contribute to our parenting skills. It's like the "Twenty Questions" game: a no is every bit as valuable as a yes because it helps us narrow the field of options. If we insist on denying any pain or suffering we may have experienced, we run the risk of unconsciously repeating painful behaviors with our children—even if we swore we never would. We have all felt wounded at times. Instead of wounding our own children, let's use our love for them as an inspiration to heal ourselves.

Give your children what you want back. If you respect and accept them, they will learn to respect and accept; if you abuse and reject them, they will learn to abuse and reject. It's like a hug: you have to give one away if you want to get one back. Children are natural imitators. They reflect how you think, how you love, what you value, how you solve problems, what you do with feelings and how you are in the world. Whether you know it or not, you are teaching self-esteem—or a lack of it—to your children all the time. So, be your best self, and they will want to become their best, too. Self-esteem in families begins with who you are.

Parenting gives you an opportunity to create joy and love. It also encourages you to develop desirable personal qualities (such as patience), to under-stand and appreciate *yourself* at deeper levels, and to learn new skills. Your children become your best teachers.

One mother, Anne, said, "My lessons began with bonding. As I held my beautiful baby, I experienced a totally unconditional love between us, and a wonderful sense of euphoria. I was aware and appreciative of my uniqueness. My twenty-two-month-old son has taught me so many lessons. He's taught me what love is, he's taught me self-acceptance, and he's taught me to relax and let him go through his stages."

As parents we need to provide a loving, safe home for our children. We also need to face the fact that our larger Home—the planet—is in crisis. Healing the planet is essential if we care about the future for our children and our children's children. This is an enormous responsibility and an exciting challenge. Working with others, we can help fashion a new, healthy world. We can raise our children to become healthy adults who will join us in creating a more positive and peaceful world for everyone.

2.

The Greatest Gift: Self-Esteem

"What a man thinks of himself, that it is which determines, or rather indicates his fate."

—Henry David Thoreau[1]

We make healthy children by working from the inside-out—by cherishing and accepting them as they are, and nurturing their growth and development. "We make butterflies by feeding caterpillars, not by trying to paste wings on them," according to Foster Cline.[2]

Self-esteem means esteeming yourself and knowing you are worthwhile. In affirming your dignity, you know you have a right to be treated with respect. You have a right to be happy. Self-esteem involves a sense of personal competence and confidence in your ability to deal with life.

It is not uncommon for people to try to gain a sense of importance by being one-up over others. This is egotism: getting a sense of importance at another's expense, for example, "I'm the best and you're not." People who feel good about themselves don't have to put others down.

Many people think that self-esteem comes from others or from something external. They may believe that someone else is responsible for their happiness. The fact is, for adults, *self*-esteem is something that you give to your*self*.

Only *you* can give yourself *self*-respect.

Only *you* can give yourself *self*-acceptance.

Only *you* can give yourself *self*-esteem.

5

Typically, people try to gain self-esteem from external sources, through

- *What they do.* Many people get their self-esteem through work or through doing things for others. They shift from being human beings to human doings. They may be workaholics.
- *What they have.* "He who dies with the most toys wins," reads a bumper sticker. Some people crave material possessions and can never get enough. Competing with the Joneses, their "stuff" and debts control their lives.
- *What they know.* Many people try to impress others with information and with the many books they have read.
- *How they perform.* Many people are acutely aware of how they affect others. They operate their lives attempting to achieve a desired effect on others.
- *How they look.* Many people put a great amount of time, effort, and money into their appearance.
- *Who they are with.* Many people think they have to have a "good" partner in order to be okay.

The ultimate hope in each of these cases is that others will notice and approve of them; *then* they will be okay. Their self-esteem is based on externals. They are people pleasers and approval seekers who have given others the power to control their self-esteem. This "self"-esteem is conditional. For example, "If I do_____, I am okay." "If I look beautiful, I am okay." "If I act_____ I am okay." Conversely, "If I don't do_____, I am not okay." Each of these things can contribute to our self-esteem. The problem arises when we *need to* impress or please others—when we are dependent on approval in order to feel okay.

Such external sources of self-esteem are not solid. I may feel okay today because I have a bigger boat than the Joneses; yet tomorrow they might buy an even better one. I may feel okay today because I've read every book on the best seller list; yet next month I may not have time. Or I may feel okay because I did a thousand things for my family; yet if I stop doing all those things (possibly because of exhaustion), then I'm not okay and my self-esteem drops.

Self-esteem is not what you do or know; it is not based on your appearance or how much money you have. *Self-esteem is based on who you are.* As you accept, respect, and cherish yourself more, you can take charge of your own self-esteem and stop working so hard to prove it by pleasing others. By becoming more pleasing to yourself, you esteem yourself more, and become more pleasing to others in the process.

Unconditional self-esteem is based on unconditional love for yourself. The First Commandment tells us to love our neighbors as ourselves. This means that we should first love ourselves, then love our neighbors (and our children). In reality, if I hate myself, I can't love my kids or my neighbor very well. And if I believe that I am not lovable, it's hard to imagine that my kids or anyone else might really love me—even when they do. It begins with a choice, plus a change of self-talk and a change of heart.

Positive self-esteem is the choice and commitment to respect, accept, and love yourself completely. It is the best gift you can give to yourself—and your child. This gift is in your hands.

Self-esteem evolves through the quality of the relationships between children and those who are important in their lives. For the most part, children look to the adults in their environment (and later to their peers) for a reflection of who they are and how they are. Keen observers, they soak up every bit of information we provide—our words, facial expressions, posture, tone of voice, touch. They notice how we react and respond to them: whether their physical and emotional needs are met, whether they are taken seriously and listened to, whether they are respected and enjoyed. They observe, then draw conclusions. ("I am important," "I don't matter," "I am loved," "I'm a nuisance.")

Their conclusions become their truth, their basic beliefs about who they are and what they deserve in life. Sometimes their conclusions are faulty. For example, children may conclude that they are responsible for their parents' divorce. Yet their perception is not true. It is merely one way of looking at things.

Children tend to view parents and authority figures as all-knowing and all-powerful. They think "Those important people treat me as I deserve to be treated. What they say about me is what I am." When children are respected, they conclude that they *deserve* respect; they develop self-respect. When they are treated with esteem, when they are cherished, they conclude that they *deserve* esteem, and they develop self-esteem. On the other hand, if they are mistreated or abused, they conclude that they deserve *that*—that they had it coming; it becomes natural for them to allow mistreatment from others.

The truth is, no one deserves abuse or harmful punishment. Every single child—every single person—deserves and needs respect, acceptance, and unconditional love. A child will ask for these naturally; a parent's job is to reflect these qualities back. Parents are, in effect, like mirrors. The reflection they give becomes the basis for their children's self-image, influencing all aspects of their lives.

Fostering self-esteem in a child from the outset is easier and healthier than trying to repair damaged self-esteem later in life. Yet we cannot turn back the clock. We must start where we are now. If your children are older, it's not too late. *The same things that build self-esteem in the first place also repair damaged self-esteem later on*—for your children and yourself. A new approach, new skills, and a dash of forgiveness can begin the healing process.

A thirty-five-year-old woman told me that she barely spoke to her mother from the time she was about eight or nine until she was twenty-six and divorcing from her first husband. Only then did they begin to share feelings, to develop a sense of trust in each other, to work through some of the misunderstandings and unintentional hurts that had come between them. Today they have a warm, supportive, and loving relationship.

It's obviously easier to develop self-esteem if you know how to go about it. Good intentions start you on the right path. Information and application (putting the ideas into practice) move you closer to your goal. As little as five minutes a day trying out new strategies with your children can produce positive changes.

So what do you do first? Self-esteem begins with self-love, with respecting, accepting, and taking care of *yourself*. That love spills over to your children, who learn to love themselves and to love you. *Love cures people—those who give it and those who receive it.*

Where does it begin with children? With bonding. This most critical and amazing developmental task occurs naturally when newborn infant and mother have skin-to-skin and other sensory contact—nursing, cooing, touching.... If permitted to do so, a newborn bonds almost immediately to mother and father. This primal attachment is the foundation for trust, for love, for self-esteem and healthy development. Through bonding with our children, we can heal incomplete bonding with our mothers. We can also re-connect with our inner child and begin a process of deep personal healing.

If you had difficulty with early bonding, or if you adopted, there are always other opportunities to form that bond—to fall in love with your child. As you take care of and care for your child, bonding can occur in more subtle ways.

Self-esteem depends on *unconditional* love: love with no strings attached; love with respect, acceptance, appreciation, empathy, sensitivity, and warmth; love that says, "Regardless of what you do, I love and accept you for who you are."

A day care provider told me about two-and-a-half year old Joey, who would say when he got in trouble, "That's okay, because my mom and dad still love me!" His parents had laid a solid, loving foundation.

Conditional love, on the other hand, is turned on and off. It manipulates behavior by saying, "I love you *when...*, *because...*, or *if* you do something." Kids who receive only conditional love never really *feel* loved; if they receive it they can't trust it. These kids try to *earn* love by becoming people pleasers.

Children have their own life force, their own opinions, dreams, and destinies. The task of parents is to allow and encourage children to be themselves while guiding, supporting, and celebrating their process of growth. Successful parenting involves not only unconditional love but also the protection, limit setting, and responsibility appropriate to the child's developmental stage. Newborn infants are totally dependent on adults for their well-being, but growing children need the freedom to *be* and *act* their age. It's important to turn over responsibility to children as they are ready. If you're helping your child across the street at three, that's great, but if he or she is fifteen, you have a problem. Let your children be silly, let them play, let them be kids while they're kids. When you understand the character of children at different ages, it makes it easier for you to work *with* their nature, not *against* it.

The letting go process is a gradual, orderly transfer of freedom and responsibility from parent to child, from birth to maturity. Through this process, children gain self-confidence, independence, and self-esteem. By the time they are young adults, they will be responsible individuals equipped with the lifeskills they need to function happily and effectively.

Pause for a moment to reflect on your own self-esteem, as a child and as an adult. Over the years you have had your ups and downs. What were the causes? Take a few minutes to write down the things that have affected your self-esteem.

Low self-esteem comes from

- rejection
- conditional love or no love at all
- lack of attention, being ignored, neglect
- not being taken seriously; not being listened to
- disrespect
- emotional abuse, e.g., put-downs, name-calling, ridicule, sarcasm,

9

blaming, humiliation, criticism, threats
- needs not being met
- prejudice
- comparison, perfectionism, always looking for what's wrong
- focusing on externals (appearances, behavior, performance)
- expectations that are too high or too low
- guilt, shame, resentment
- physical and sexual abuse or exploitation.

Remember that when children experience this kind of treatment, they conclude, "I'm not important." "I can't do things right." "I'm not good enough." "I'm not okay." This becomes their Truth, and their self-esteem plunges.

On the other hand, **high self-esteem** comes from

- acceptance, respect, love
- attention, being taken seriously and listened to
- a feeling of connectedness, belonging, bonding
- honesty (with tact and sensitivity), integrity
- having needs taken seriously and met
- honoring uniqueness
- authentic expression of feelings
- encouragement, support, appreciation, believing in
- safety, security
- high and attainable expectations
- competence, success, achievement
- doing good and being good
- a sense of personal power; having choices
- personal and social responsibility
- being healthy and fit
- affectionate and appropriate touch
- forgiveness; allowing and learning from mistakes
- having meaning in life, a sense of purpose
- living up to one's own moral standards
- a sense of connection with a Higher Power (spirituality)
- gratitude
- laughter and play.

As children observe and experience these positive influences in their lives, they conclude: "I'm okay." "I'm glad to be me." "Mom and Dad think I'm important. I must matter." "I'm worthwhile." "I'm loved." Their self-esteem soars. If you stop doing the things that lower self-esteem and do more and more of the things that raise self-esteem, you will notice marked improvements in your family relations. Low self-esteem cannot be "fixed". Over time, however, you can help it to heal.

I recently realized that when I'm behaving from the low self-esteem mode, my kids feel bad, *and so do I.* On the other hand, when I'm operating from high self-esteem, everyone's self-esteem increases! When I'm good to them, we all come out winning, and when I'm nasty, we suffer. For better or worse, self-esteem is contagious.

The essence of self-esteem is compassion for yourself and for your children. With compassion you understand and accept yourself. When you make a mistake you forgive yourself. And you do the same for your kids.

Needs vs. Problems

Plants need good soil, water, and sunshine to flourish. In order to thrive, children also need optimal growing conditions. First and foremost, they need unconditional love. They also need to feel safe at home and at school; they need to know they will not be harmed. They need to feel secure about the future and not constantly worry about what is going to happen. It is the job of the family to meet the needs of children. If children's needs are not met, there will be problems.

If you ignore the needs of your houseplants—soil, water, sunshine—your plants might die. If your car needs gasoline and you don't get it, you'll obviously have problems. If your house needs roof repair and you don't take care of it, you'll be in trouble with the next downpour. Either we tend to needs or we have problems.

Children (and adults) have basic physical needs: they must have shelter and food to eat. They also have emotional needs which must be met: love and respect, acceptance and understanding, support and encouragement, affection and belonging; and security (which comes from structure, freedom, and predictability). Meeting these needs will insure their physical and emotional well-being. They will thrive. Ignore them and you (and your children) will have problems. Tending to the basics when children are young can prevent pain, grief, and expensive therapy when they are older. An ounce of prevention is worth (at least) a pound of cure.

Families that do not meet basic needs are dysfunctional families. The persons society labels "sick", according to the late Abraham Maslow, have never had their basic human needs met—or they had, then lost that need satisfaction.

What is the best medicine then? "For a child who hasn't been loved enough", wrote Maslow, "obviously the treatment of first choice is to love him..., just slop it all over him. Clinical and general human experience is that it works." This also holds true for adults. The same things that build high self-esteem in the first place can heal the damage later on.

If your emotional development was stunted as a kid, there's hope! Healing is possible. And as you fill in your own developmental holes, you can become whole—and will be better equiped to nurture the development of your children.

Self-Esteem Building Exercise

Get a partner to do this with you. Sit facing each other. One person, A, looks the other, B, in the eyes and says, "Tell me how you're terrific!" That's the only thing that A says.

B responds by saying, "I'm terrific because. . ." and completes the sentence. B repeats this sentence with different endings for three or four minutes. At the end of this time you switch roles.

After you both have taken a turn, talk about it. How was it to hear those terrific things about your partner? How was it to say those terrific things about yourself?

Many people get embarrassed because they haven't thought of themselves in terms of terrificness. Many feel as if they're bragging. Yet Will Rogers said, "If it's the truth, it can't be bragging." "Flip" your focus from negative to positive.

Helen, a grandmother attending a workshop, shared her awareness after the exercise: "I got in touch with my roots—with who I really am. I went back to the joy of the little girl I used to be—before I was contaminated with the negative messages of growing up."

Start catching yourself—and your kids—being terrific. You are terrific—and so are they. *Whatever you look for, you find.* Then tell them about it. Positive thoughts are a beginning, just as a basket of flower seeds is a beginning. The next step, however, is to plant those seeds in their hearts so they can blossom. They need more appreciation. Give it to them. *What you focus on expands.*

Look also for the stengths in your family. Too often, people focus on the weaknesses and take their positive qualities for granted. They need an attitude adjustment. Talk about your family strengths, then give each other appreciation and hugs. There's something sacred about a family. A lot of esteem is built into creating a secure and nurturing home for the people we love.

3.

Self-Esteem Protection Skills

"No one can make you feel inferior without your consent."

—Eleanor Roosevelt[1]

The bumper sticker on the blue sports car in front of me reads: "If you're cute, honk. If you're not, bark." The put-down startles me. This is but one small example of the cruelty people inflict so carelessly on strangers, acquaintances, and members of their own families. Negativity is so common that it almost seems normal in our culture. Like pollution, it creeps into our homes and under our skin. We have to be aware of toxic levels in our environment and our systems, lest our self-esteem is damaged.

As children we learn quickly that the world can be full of downers: school days are filled with chances for humiliation. Typical self-esteem eaters kids encounter daily are: being put down by peers, embarrassed by teachers, and abused by bullies; wearing the wrong clothes to school, getting poor grades, dropping the ball in P.E., and forgetting important things at home; awkwardness around the opposite sex, not knowing where you belong, and not understanding what's being asked of you.

Hopefully, by the time we've reached adulthood we've begun to learn how to keep these things from sending our self-esteem into a tailspin.

Everyone—children and adults alike—needs strategies for *increasing* self-esteem and strategies for *protecting* their self-esteem from bullies and toxic people and situations. The most important thing you can do in your daily life is to keep self-esteem high—and the most important thing you can do for your kids is teach them to protect and nurture their own high self-esteem. Self-esteem carries its own momentum—the more you have, the less time you need to spend putting your pieces back together.

Think of a time when your self-esteem was really high and someone flung an insult your way. In your confidence you let it go right past, thinking they didn't know what they were talking about. The better you feel about yourself, the less vulnerable you are to negativity. Remember, on the other hand, a time your self-esteem was sagging and someone gave you a compliment. You may have denied it, or found yourself looking between the lines for "what they really meant".

But if someone offers us a plate of garbage, do we say, "No thanks" and go on our way? or do we take it anyway because we don't know how to say no?

Here are some strategies both you and your children can use for dealing with daily slings and arrows:

- **Inquire.** Asking, "Is something wrong?" or "What do you mean by that?" throws the responsibility back on the insult-giver and invites them to talk about it. Perhaps there was some miscommunication.
- **Confront.** You don't need to grin and bear it, or be a martyr. If a put-down hurts you, you might say "Ouch" or "I don't like that". Children can also use the "snake sound"—hissing at the person and pointing two fingers like the tongue of a threatened, dangerous snake. This may be easier for kids than defending themselves verbally. Some classroom teachers teach this to their students, putting them on the alert for put-downs to themselves and others.
- **Withdraw.** We don't want to be around people who are nasty, cruel or annoying. This can be a lifesaver in some cases. But be careful—don't overuse this one.
- **Don't take it personally.** Mostly kids and other people do things for themselves, not against you. Maybe they're having a bad day. Maybe they're unaware or simply careless. The put-down probably has nothing to do with you. Instead of reacting, you might act to find out what's underneath the barb.
- **Humor.** As the shortest kid in his class, Joe was sometimes called "Shrimp". He'd look them right in the eyes, smile, and say, "Hmm, I love shrimp."
- **Make a neutral remark.** When they finish, say, "Oh," or, "I see."
- **Consider the source.** Some people seem to wallow in negativity. Let them express whatever emotions they choose and know that they have little or nothing to do with you.
- **Disagree.** Realize that what they're saying is just their opinion; you know yourself better than they do.
- **Sift through.** Perhaps there is some truth in what they're saying but they haven't yet learned good, gentle feedback skills.
- **Call a friend.** A shoulder to cry on can comfort and strengthen you.

- **Use positive self-talk.** Repeat over and over to yourself, "No matter what you say or do to me, I'm still a worthwhile person."[2] Teach these strategies to your kids and to anyone you know who is in a toxic or abusive situation. It will help them protect the inner core of their confidence and self-worth.

Here are strategies that have worked for other people:

- **"Wax your back."** A dear friend of mine once told me that every morning he waxes his back and his life is great. No, it isn't to rid himself of superfluous hair, it's a metaphor to protect him from whatever negativity might "rain" on him in the business world, just as oily feathers protect a duck. He takes preventive measures to safeguard his self-esteem.
- **Give yourself a hug.** Give one to your kid. Hugs are great for a send-off in the morning, a welcome home later on or an affectionate good-night. Life goes better with hugs!
- **Clothing and jewelry.** Wonder Woman had bracelets and a "golden girdle." People wear "power" clothes when they want to make a powerful impression—when, for example, they want to borrow money from a bank. A piece of jewelry or a special garment, (maybe Batman underwear) can give a sense of personal strength and power.

- **Permission to be different.** Kids (and adults!) often get a lot of pressure to be like everyone else. They get teased because they are wearing the "wrong" clothes. If you teach them that they are unique and don't have to act and dress like everyone else, they'll be less affected by those pressures. Give them permission to be different—to be who they really are.

You don't have to put up with put downs. You don't have to be a toxic waste dump. Try these strategies, or some of your own, until you find some that work for you, that help you maintain your self-esteem. Help your kids do the same and add to the *positive* energy in this world!

4.

"I Know They Love Me, But I Don't Feel It."

"The remarkable thing is that we really love our neighbor as ourselves: we do unto others as we do unto ourselves. We hate others when we hate ourselves. We are tolerant toward others when we tolerate ourselves. We forgive others when we forgive ourselves. It is not love of self but hatred of self which is at the root of the troubles that afflict our world."

—Eric Hoffer[1]

On their twenty-fifth wedding anniversary, a wife told her husband that she had been showing her love all those years by warming his plates for him. He replied, "I hate having warm plates!" Apparently they then were able to work through this miscommunication because they went on to celebrate their thirtieth anniversary—probably with cold plates.

There are two parts to communication: sending the message and receiving it. Most parents probably love their children, but because of personal shortcomings and faulty communication styles, children do not feel loved. Their self-esteem suffers needlessly.

In my workshops I ask parents how many *knew* while growing up that they were loved by their parents; many hands usually go up. Then I ask how many *felt* loved; fewer hands are raised.

Sometimes parents who really love their children don't know how to convey that love; sometimes the children don't know how to accept it. A parent of a teenage bulimic confessed, "My daughter never felt loved, but I loved her very much!" Being loved does not necessarily mean feeling loved. Yet feeling loved is the first and most fundamental need of a child.

In our society, many men are taught from childhood not to express their feelings. Having learned to block out difficult feelings, they unfortunately also blocked out the beautiful feeling of love. Shere Hite's

17

survey of seven-thousand men revealed that almost none of them were close to their fathers. Raising children was often considered "woman's work," and fathers working away from home for long hours had little contact with their kids.

One survey revealed that fathers spent an average of thirty-seven seconds a day interacting with their infants. Another showed a marked decrease in contact after a divorce: by early adolescence, 50 percent of the children from divorced families had *no* contact with their dads, 30 percent had *sporadic* contact, and only 20 percent saw their fathers *once* a week or more.[2] Yet children need their dads as well as their moms. They need to connect deeply—emotionally—with them. They need to hear "I love you" and *feel* loved by them. And dads need to love and feel loved by their children.

What did you get from your Dad? What did you *want* from your Dad? What you wanted is probably what your children need and want from you.

If you did not learn to love as a child, now is the time. Kids are perfect to start on. They're receptive and responsive, and can teach you what love is. Learn to receive love, to love yourself. Then you can more easily nurture, love, and parent your children.

"If we cannot love ourselves, where will we draw our love for anyone else?"
—Newman and Berkowitz[3]

What *Does Not* Communicate Love

There has been much harm done in the name of love. Parents with good intentions try to show their love in many ways that don't work, such as the following:

- **Overpermissiveness.** Parents think, "My kids know that I love them because I let them do anything they want." A high school friend of mine who could stay out as late as she wanted came to the conclusion that her parents didn't care enough to set a curfew. Children need safe, healthy and reasonable limits; our willingness to set those limits conveys love.
- **Martyrdom.** Many women were taught to be self-sacrificing—continually giving to others without taking care of themselves. They set aside their own needs, believing that was the way to express love for their families. Many ended up as martyrs and doormats. By putting themselves last, they came to feel resentful and depleted, and their children did not feel loved. These

parents did too much for their children—things that the children should have been doing for themselves (including solving problems), which deprived the children of the opportunity to learn, gain confidence, and build their self-esteem. These children came to expect that someone else would always "do it for them." It is important for parents to take care of themselves, to see to their own needs. Then they will have more to give to those they love.

- **Overprotection.** In this sometimes scary world we live in, our children need to be protected from danger and harm. However, if we overprotect them, they conclude that they aren't capable.
- **Material possessions.** Linda, a thirty-six-year-old mom told me, "My father would buy me anything I wanted, but he would never hug me or show me any affection. I've spent my whole life feeling that he didn't love me." Instead of presents, give your children your presence. (If you buy less you can work fewer hours.) *The best thing to spend on your children is your time.*
- **Quantity time without quality**. Spending lots of time together does not necessarily communicate love. Many people raised by adults who were with them twenty-four hours a day felt unloved. Kids need a great deal of our time for daily attention and care. With new skills, parents can increase the quality and mutual enjoyment of that time together.

What *Does* Communicate Love

Larry, an older man in my workshop, said, "I felt loved when my dad carried me on his shoulders and sang to me." One woman felt loved when the family built an ice rink and then went skating together. The love in their families increased, as did the self-esteem. It was great fun that created those endearing memories.

Take a few moments and ask yourself what situations made you feel loved as a child. Are you doing things like that for or with your children?

There are many ways we can communicate love effectively to children, including:

- **Taking them seriously.** The things that happen in your children's lives are of tremendous importance to them. Put yourself in their shoes and value what they share with you.
- **Really listening.** This is one of the most basic and important lifeskills and will be discussed in the next chapter.
- **Being with, not doing for.** It's easy to get caught up in always

doing things for children. Yet it's important, at times, to put aside all the busyness and just be there with them. This is especially true in times of crisis. When children (and others) feel this quality of presence, they conclude, "It's important for you to be with me. I must matter. I am loved." Their self-esteem goes up—and so does yours.

How can we communicate to children that they are worthwhile and valuable?

- Non-verbal messages. Positive facial expressions, eye contact, loving touch and attentiveness make others feel important.
- Positive words. Everyone wants to hear good things about themselves. Make sure your words are sincere.
- Respect and enjoyment. Children read our attitudes. When we have fun with them, everybody wins.

"If everyone had just one single person in his life to say, 'I will love you no matter what. I will love you if you are stupid, if you slip and fall on your face, if you do the wrong thing, if you make mistakes, if you behave like a human being—I will love you no matter,' then we'd never end up in mental institutions."

—Leo Buscaglia[4]

5.

Listening Skills

*"To the depth that I am willing to reveal myself to you,
to that depth can I know myself."*

— John Powell[1]

Kids who grew up under the "children should be seen and not heard" rule had a distinct handicap. They were deprived of the opportunity to express their thoughts and opinions and to gain confidence in their own abilities. Many of them came to believe that what they had to say wasn't important, that they weren't important, or even that no one cared about them. Their self-esteem suffered.

The first time I felt really listened to, I was about seventeen years old. I spent the night at my friend Annie's home. She and I talked and talked into the early morning. Annie cared about what I had to say and really listened to me! I felt surprise, relief, joy, and closeness. Really listening expresses interest and caring. It is a powerful and intimate experience that enhances self-esteem and friendship.

Remember a time when you had something very important to say but the person you were talking to was *not* listening well; the listener either wasn't interested, or didn't know how to listen, or perhaps it was just a bad time to bring up that particular subject. What was that like for you? What did you feel?

Some people feel rejected, angry, unimportant, worthless, or unloved when they're not heard; they may want to close off or withdraw. Carl Jung once said that people are in institutions because no one would listen to their stories.

Communication skills are the most basic, important skills that we need in life. Without them we are doomed to continual frustration, misunderstandings, and loneliness. Since the intrusion of television into family time—when people sit back passively and ignore each other—communication patterns have changed dramatically, and many vital skills have been lost. Wendy Sarkissian, an Australian social planner who conducted extensive research in the suburbs of New South Wales, stated, "My view is that whole generations of women are being lost to us.... I've talked to women who've lived for four and a half years across the street from other women and have never even introduced themselves because they seem to have lost the skills of getting to know people, the skills of operating comfortably with other women or with other people."[2] Communication skills allow us to develop friendships and deep love relationships that enrich our lives and enhance our families.

A friend recently returned from a two-month stay in a village in northern Thailand where there was no electricity or telephone service. Every evening the family built a fire outside the home and sat around it talking with each other for two hours. Everyone in that culture naturally learns to tell stories and to listen. Having no written language, the transmission of their cultural history depends on the people's communication skills.

In our culture, few people are taught to listen, yet active listening skills aren't difficult to learn. Once you learn to use them and teach them to others, they will transform your relationships and raise self-esteem.

- *Be interested. Look interested.* Look into the eyes of the speaker. (When listening to children, sit or crouch down to be at their level.) Face the speaker directly; if you are both sitting, lean forward slightly.
- *Put aside judgment and criticism.* Get into their experience and feelings; get inside their shoes and try to understand what happened. Put yourself and your own concerns aside; don't be thinking about what you'll say next.
- *Be aware of non-verbal cues.* Note the speed and inflection of the voice; the sighs and gulps; posture; the eyes glazing over or tearing. Reading between the lines gives you important information.
- *Let them finish.* Don't interrupt. While you are the listener, let the speaker do the talking. At times it may be okay to briefly interject something *if* it enhances the other's story. The speaker has the ball; do not take it away. This may be difficult for those who are used to communicating competitively—impatiently waiting for a comma, then jumping in. There's a reason God gave us two ears and one mouth. Put your total attention on the speaker. You'll get your turn afterward.

If you have actively listened, you have gathered much information. You noticed body language; you probably figured out the feelings involved—you know what you would have felt if this had happened to you.

- *Reflect the feeling(s)* back to the other person, from his or her point of view. For example, "I bet you were scared," or "You must

22

have been really excited," or "You must feel _____ because
_____."[3] A direct response to them about their experience com-
pletes their communication.

If you reflected accurately, the speaker will probably breathe a sigh of
relief at being understood or perhaps will exclaim excitedly, "Yes,
that's right!" If you have not reflected accurately, the speaker has an
opportunity to clear the misunderstanding. The need for a response is
so important that little children can repeat a statement over and over
and over again until the parent comments. The response lets them
know that they were heard. The transaction is complete.

The conversation can then take one of several turns. The listener
can help the speaker explore the situation ("Would you do it that way
again?") or offer guidance ("How can I help you?"). Then the listener
can speak, expanding upon that topic or telling another story.

Like a tennis match, good communication involves give and take.
Taking turns is only fair. It is essential for mutual satisfaction and
enjoyment.

Some speakers tend to derail and wander off the topic. Both
speaker and listener should pay attention to tracking, and also to the
deeper issues.

Practice active listening with someone. Find a time that is convenient for both. Read this section together, then take turns being the
speaker and the listener, each talking for about two or three minutes.
Afterward, discuss how it felt. Did you really feel listened to? If not,
what might your partner have done differently so that you would feel
listened to? Give feedback in a positive way; for example, "When I
noticed your arms were folded, I thought you weren't interested in
what I had to say. I would appreciate it if you didn't fold your arms
when you listen to me."

If, as the speaker, you were really listened to, you probably experienced some or all of these feelings: excitement, interest, a sense of
closeness to the listener, validation, self-worth, understanding, love.
As a listener you probably felt interest, trust, enrichment from a new
experience, excitement, and closeness to the speaker. You have given
a great gift. Self-esteem on both sides has increased. This is *win-win
communication.*

Think back to the time when you felt you weren't being heard.
Who came out winning? No one.

Good listening skills are as difficult to learn as driving a car. They
need to be practiced. At first they may feel awkward and artificial.
That's okay. Keep at it, and they'll get easier. After a while they will be
automatic. Like driving, it becomes second nature—and is just as
effective for getting from place to place!

Good listeners take the time to listen. They help people discover that they have stories to tell. Good listening keeps people healthy and happy. It's an important skill that will improve the quality of your family life, your relationships and everyone's self-esteem. There's a reason that we have two ears and only one mouth.

"If you take time to talk together each day, you'll never become strangers."

—Leo Buscaglia[4]

6.

Asking and Refusal Skills

"So much to say. And so much not to say!
Some things are better left unsaid.
But so many unsaid things can become a burden."

—Virginia Mae Axline[1]

To ride a bicycle, you must know how to make it go and stop, and how to make it turn. Communication skills are just as basic. You need sending skills to let others know what you want and don't want. You need listening skills for understanding, for resolving differences, for closeness, and for love.

There are three basic ways people use to get what they want: monster ways, mouse ways, and assertive ways.[2]

Monster ways include shouting, venting anger recklessly, hitting, manipulating, and intimidating others. *Mouse ways* include crying, whining, begging, pouting, hinting, and hoping someone will read your mind ("If he really loves me, he'll know what I want!" This works only if he or she is psychic.) Monster and mouse communication styles may work, but they usually create bad feelings in the process. Remember a time you yelled or cried all day, then got what you wanted. Was there any sweetness in getting it?

Stereotypically, females are taught the passive communication style; males are taught the aggressive communication style. Then, traditionally, we take one of each, put them together, and tell them to live happily ever after!

The best way to communicate is by *assertive ways*. This involves knowing what you want and then asking or telling others: "Would you help me?" "I don't like it when you..." "I'd really like to get together more often." "Please give me a hug."

Instead of complaining about how hard you work, for example, and how ungrateful everyone is, say, "I worked very hard today and would like some applause, appreciation, flowers, or hugs." When we ask for

what we want, we are much more likely to get it; unlike mouse and monster communication styles, asking does not cause residual negativity. Do remember to be sensitive to the timing of the question/request.

Asking is a powerful tool for creating positive self-esteem. It is not a sign of weakness or failure, but a tool for helping you get your needs met. Sometimes it's hard to know what you want, so pay attention to your feelings. Follow your anger to its roots. Listen to your fears and their message. Tune in to your desires and wishes.

Asking may feel strange at first, but it will get easier. Asking for what you want and need takes practice. It can be difficult or intimidating at first, but it is worth the risk. Openness leads to honesty which can be very rewarding.

It's okay to get what you want. Allow yourself to receive. You deserve it. Let others help you. This, in turn, can give you the strength to help others.

We can ask questions to express interest and caring for others. Open-ended questions ("Would you tell me about your day?") encourage more talking than questions that can be answered with one word or a phrase ("How are you?" "Fine."). To improve communication, ask, "How do you feel about...?" "What do you want?" "How can I help?" Asking, in a respectful tone of voice, can lead to greater understanding.

Teaching children to ask empowers them to get their needs met. Young children who know how to ask for a glass of water, for example, don't have to whine or cry or act out in other undesirable ways to get their thirst quenched. Direct asking can make life much easier for parents. You don't have to try to read their minds.

In general, directly asking is easier with people who know how to say no. If they can't or won't say no, we second-guess and make assumptions about what we think will make them happy, about what they will or will not like.

Everyone also needs to be able to say no. As adults, "no" lets us set limits for our children and ourselves. It helps us maintain integrity. Children also need to be able to say no. Sadly, the media is filled with stories of children being manipulated and exploited in unhealthy ways. As youngsters, children need to learn that their bodies belong to them alone and that they have the right to say no to anyone who might try to touch them. Older children need to learn to say no to drugs, alcohol, and promiscuous sex. If they have not been taught refusal skills, children will be vulnerable to pressure and manipulation, to pitfalls and dangers.

Saying no, like braking on a bicycle, lets us stop what we don't want and get more of what we do want. "It is not okay to say no, however," writes author Patricia Palmer, "if it is a responsibility or something you have agreed to do. And remember, how you say no makes a difference. Treat others as you like to be treated."[3]

Many people have great difficulty saying no. If this is a problem for you, complete this sentence several times: "Saying no means...." Allow yourself to become aware of why it is difficult for you to say no.

One of the reasons people have difficulty saying no is that they have negative associations with the word. Perhaps you find this true of yourself. For many people, saying no means rejection, selfishness, guilt, failure, weakness, stubbornness, hurting others' feelings, not being liked by others, risking anger.... No wonder they have such difficulties!

Now think of the *value* of saying no.[4] Write your thoughts down before reading further.

Saying no is like giving yourself a present—of honesty, freedom (you don't feel used), relief, authority, peace, power, confidence, and integrity. It establishes boundaries. It gives you self-definition and self-respect. It gives you time and control over your own life. It makes your yeses more meaningful.

Sometimes parents threaten their kids saying, "I'm going to spank you." A much better word choice to stop unacceptable behavior is a simple, firm no, or stop. As parents we must say no when our child's health or safety is at risk. Like anything else, however, no can be overused, rendering it ineffective (like the boy who cried wolf). Say yes at least three times more often than no. When you say no, sound serious; lower the tone of your voice. Look serious; a smile may confuse them. Say no with respect and firmness. Avoid being nasty. *You don't have to be mean to mean business.*

One summer, for example, my eighteen-year-old son Felix, told me he wanted to learn sky diving with his friends. I laughed (probably out of nervousness), then joked about it ("Well, Felix, do you have insurance?"). Then I firmly said, "No, you may not do it. I love you and want to enjoy you for many more years to come." He and his buddies went to the airport to watch what was going on, and after seeing the setup, he realized that he didn't even want to do it.

Kids need to explore the world and learn about life. Guide them in this process of discovery while keeping in mind their age and developmental needs. Toddlers, for example, need to touch. Instead of saying no all the time to my first two babies (born eleven months apart), I put my special things out of reach and allowed them to touch other objects with only one finger. They satisfied their need to reach out and explore without the risk of destruction.

Women face additional difficulty in saying no because of the myth that when she says no she really means yes. When women say no, men may not take them seriously, and thereby disempower them. Certainly many cases of date-rape have resulted from this communication tangle. If this is very difficult for you, consider going to a therapist or an assertiveness class to learn how to say no.

People who talk and listen to others can form and maintain healthy, happy relationships. They can share ideas, opinions, and feelings without fearing judgment and criticism. Learning and practicing communication skills increases understanding, trust, openness, closeness, and love between people—and everyone's self-esteem goes up.

7.

Dealing with Feelings

*"It is terribly amusing how many different climates of feeling
I can go through in one day."*

—Anne Morrow Lindbergh[1]

Everyone is born with a full deck of capabilities—physical, intellectual, spiritual, & emotional. We need to learn to play them well in order to become healthy, fully functioning individuals. Often though, there are some cards—some aspects of ourselves—that we don't know how to deal with. We may unconsciously pass on our own limitations to the feelings of our children. Yet, children must learn to deal with their own feelings if they are to live their own lives fully and freely.

"Say you're sorry!" "Tell me you love me." "You should be happy." "Don't be mad." "You don't really feel that way." It's easy to try to force feelings on others. Yet when parents dictate or manipulate kids' feelings, they pressure them to give up their own emotional reality. Kids cannot do this; they can't manufacture emotions. With you-shouldn't-feel-how-you-feel messages, kids conclude that their feelings are unacceptable, wrong, or even nonexistent. They conclude that they can't trust others with their feelings or, perhaps, that they can't trust their own feelings.

Not knowing what to do with their emotions, children hide them—from themselves and others—or deny them altogether. They become isolated in fear, worry, embarrassment, anger, or guilt. They build protective walls around themselves that increase isolation. They repress their true feelings yet pretend to feel different.[2]

"Safety disappears, when you decide what children 'should' enjoy"—or feel. "Respect for separateness proves you care," writes author Dorothy Corkille Briggs. Everyone has a right to his or her own feelings. And this right must be accepted and protected. Kids have their own bodies, their own minds, their own dreams, and their own feelings. They are unique individuals, different from you. "Your way of seeing and feeling is not the only way of seeing and feeling," writes Briggs.

It can be hard to accept kids' feelings—especially if we have trouble with our own. Allowing and getting comfortable with your feelings can help you re-parent yourself as you parent your child. When you accept children's emotions—whatever they may be—you help them to "own" their feelings. They conclude, "My feelings are okay even when they're not the same as my dad's," "It's okay to be me," "I'm okay." Self-esteem goes up when you honor differences.

Feelings are valid: listen to them. Take a deep breath. When we have feelings we can't handle, we hold our breath. When we breathe through them, we release them. Inhale. Exhale. Repeat. Feelings that have been "stuffed" for a long time may become distorted and exaggerated. Accept them. Allow them to be. They are okay. Allow *yourself* to feel the pain, the anger, even the hatred that might be inside. Acknowledging these feelings is the first step toward releasing and resolving them.

Feelings have a legitimate purpose. They are part of being human and must be accepted. "Feelings seem inappropriate only when they are not understood," states author Claudia Black.[3] All feelings are okay. What you do with your feelings—your behavior—can be judged as acceptable or unacceptable.

If you share your feelings openly, children and others understand you more and don't have to rely on guesswork to know what's happening. In expressing feelings you might say, "I feel mad/glad/sad because...," and then ask for what you want. Talking things out can release internal pressures, help you get perspective, and open you to the support and caring of others. Not talking about your feelings can create anxiety, tension, and distance. *You teach your children how to handle their feelings by how you handle yours.*

When children get hurt, encourage them to say, "Ow." If a physician is giving a shot and it hurts, saying "Ouch!" can help release the pain. This lets others know how they feel. Encourage them to ask for what they want (a kiss, perhaps, or a bandaid).

When we repress feelings tension builds up in our bodies. This pressure may be turned against the self—in the form of psychosomatic or psychological problems—or it may be directed against others in the family or in society.

What kinds of feelings did your parents express? How did they express them? What did they do with other feelings? Whose pattern do you tend to follow?

Feelings are private, internal experiences that tell us about our world, help us make decisions, and form values. They are normal, natural responses to experiences. We can react, knee-jerk fashion, to thoughts, experiences, and feelings, or we can *decide* how to respond.

Feelings can also follow our thoughts (self-talk). Fearful thoughts, for example, lead to feelings of fear, which lead to a certain set of behaviors. If, walking home at night, I worry about getting mugged, my body tenses; my breath gets shallow; expecting trouble, I walk faster. If, on the other hand, I'm thinking about how happy I'll be to get home and see my kids, I feel happy; my feet might skip in eagerness to get there. Thoughts lead to feelings which influence behavior.

When your child thinks of an ice cream cone, that creates a desire which leads to certain behaviors intended to get him or her a cone. If you choose not to buy one, you could.

- Deny your child's feelings ("You don't really want an ice cream cone")
- Manipulate his or her feelings ("You shouldn't feel that way before dinner").

Or you could

- Accept and acknowledge the feelings ("You'd sure like to get a cone right now"), then
- Intervene at the thought level ("But it's too close to dinnertime and might spoil your appetite"), or
- Intervene at the behavior level ("Sorry. We can't get one right now, honey").

A journal is a wonderful tool for sorting through confusion, for releasing tension, for learning to deal with emotions. This evening, list the emotions you felt during the day. When did you feel them? Where in your body did you experience them? How did you express them? Did they remind you of anything? What feelings were missing? As you clarify your feelings, you can identify patterns in your emotional processes that will help you to change and grow. A journal can start you and your children on the path to becoming your own best friend.

Trust

A child wonders: "Is this world a friendly, safe place for me?" "Can I depend on being fed when I'm hungry, on being comforted when I hurt or am frightened?" "Are my needs fulfilled?" "Can I count on my parents?" The child concludes "I can trust" or "I cannot trust."

Trust has been defined as an act of faith, belief in the other, confidence, predictability, absence of fear, feeling safe, the basis for intimacy. In order for trust to develop, children must feel safe. Parents must create a safe environment for their children. In creating safety, parents lay the foundation for trust and health.

"The single most important ingredient in a nurturing relationship—in any relationship—is honesty," states author Claudia Black. No one can trust, or be expected to trust, unless people openly and honestly talk about what's important and about their feelings. This doesn't mean, though, that you have to say everything that's on your mind. Dishonesty creates confusion and destroys trust. If you do not tell the truth, neither will your kids. They learn from you. Children want honesty. Let's resurrect the old saying, "Honesty is the best policy."

A classmate once told me: "My parents encouraged us to say anything we wanted to each other. But we had to be careful *how* we said it." She learned early in life how to be truthful, sensitive, and tactful.

When a baby is born, parents often start playing mom and dad roles. They become less of who they really are—themselves—and more of who they think they're *supposed* to be according to the models and myths they've learned. Yet, when parents aren't being genuine human beings, children find it difficult to know them or trust them.

"In a very serious way, this transformation is unfortunate because it so often results in parents forgetting they are still humans with human faults, persons with personal limitations, real persons with real feelings. Forgetting the reality of their own humanness..., they frequently cease to be human."

—T. Gordon [4]

The same holds true when parents maintain a facade of perfectionism, for example—when a "perfect" family appearance has a higher priority than having loving, solid relationships within one. The unrealistic or impossible expectations breed disappointment and distrust (See Chapter 19).

Distrust can also result from disrespect, fear, neglect, insensitivity, ridicule, humiliation, rejection, and abuse. These things can happen when trust is not consciously cultivated.

I used to think that trust was like being pregnant—all or nothing, with no in-between. Then I learned differently. We can't trust anyone 100 percent of the time. Using good judgment, we must figure out how far and in what situations we can trust people. At what age can you trust your child to carry a cup of water? When are they old enough to cross the street by themselves? When are they ready to babysit? The art of parenting and our wisdom come into play with day-to-day decisions.

Trust can be built in a variety of ways:

- Treat them with respect and caring.
- Accept them for who they are. Honor differences.
- Meet their needs. Feed them when they're hungry; see that they get enough sleep. Help them feel safe.
- Comfort them when they're afraid. Hold them when they're hurting.
- Avoid unpleasant surprises. Create a familiar, predictable, comfortable routine.
- Don't make promises you won't keep. If you won't do it, don't tell they you will.
- Spend comfortable, quality time together. Be there for them.
- Let them know they can count on you. Tell them when and where you are going and when you'll return.
- Prepare them in advance for big events in their lives. Let them know what to expect.[5]

Kids need to be able to trust their parents. And parents need to be able to trust their kids. Who do we trust? We trust people who are trust-worthy. We must be trustworthy for our kids and for ourselves.

Sometimes trust begins with a leap of faith on the part of the parents—a gift of respect, of believing in their children. With this comes high expectations. Wanting to live up to your expectations, kids become trustworthy. For this reason, we have an obligation to trust them so that they become trustworthy. We need to focus on their strong points, build on them, encourage them to be their best.

We also need to learn to trust ourselves more, thereby modeling trustworthiness. Doing this we create an environment where safety and honesty, connectedness and love can flourish. Relationships in families call for the greatest possible amount of trust.

> *"I think we may safely trust a good deal more than we do."*
>
> —Henry David Thoreau[6]

Guilt

Excessive guilt destroys self-esteem and cripples lives with anxiety. It prevents people from learning from their mistakes. Re-framing guilt—or finding another way of looking at it—can help them to understand it, accept themselves more, and begin to release its negative grip.

Guilt has been defined as moral self-disapproval. There are two types of guilt: general and specific.[7]

General guilt refers to total self-condemnation. "I am a bad person." "I am worthless." "I am evil." It is condemnation of the whole person—who they are—not of a specific act or behavior—what they did. It is very painful.

General guilt occurs in persons who do not yet have a self-defined set of values and moral standards, but who have a "secondhand" value system from parents, significant others, their church. Wanting to do what they are "supposed" to do, yet failing, these external-locus-of-control people have low self-esteem. (See Chapter 21.)

Specific guilt refers to one specific reproachful action. "I did something which was unworthy of me. I violated *my* standards." "I acted in good faith, but had an error of knowledge or judgment." When the mistake is corrected and forgiven, the guilt is released. This limited guilt is experienced by internal-locus-of-control persons who have self-defined principles by which they live.

Parents may instill deep feelings of guilt or shame to change children's behavior. They may inadvertently, however, create psychological problems for their children.

One forty-eight-year-old woman stated, "I wasted my childhood tormented with guilt and fear. I tried so hard to be good, yet I always felt bad. I tried to second-guess my mom all the time so I could avoid being blamed and criticized. I was a good little girl who grew up paralyzed by fear and guilt. If, driving down the street, I'd see a policeman, I'd feel an intense wave of anxiety even though I had done nothing wrong! It took me years to get rid of the shackles of guilt and fear."

Statements that influence behavior while manipulating feelings include

- "I'm very disappointed in you."
- "How could you do this to me?"
- "Shame on you."
- "Don't get hurt! Be careful! Don't fall!"
- "I love you when you_____." "I love you if you_____."

Children who grow up hearing these messages tend to be insecure and scared. They may feel guilty about everything.

Many parents see unacceptable behavior, then overgeneralize; they don't deal with the *one specific thing* that the kid did wrong, but they confuse the issue by saying, "*You* are a bad person." They may blow it out of proportion saying, "I can't believe that you would have even thought to do that!" If the kid was doing his or her best and trying to be good, the parents' response can be baffling. More likely, the kid wasn't thinking about what he or she did—not in the way adults think. Feeling confused and not quite understanding what went wrong, the child might become reluctant to do *anything* for fear of displeasing the parents. This type of paralysis can "freeze" a child's development; the child may come to distrust himself or herself, and suffer intensely from guilt and low self-esteem.

It's okay for a child to feel bad about doing a bad thing. But the child should not end up feeling like an awful person. The desired outcome is fixing whatever is wrong, learning from the mistake, and not repeating it. The child thinks, "I did a bad/stupid thing, but I'm still a good person." Finally, forgiveness completes and heals it.

People who feel excessive guilt probably suffer from generalized guilt. Here are some ways you can deal with it:

- Minimize it. Ask yourself, What one specific action is the cause of the guilt?
- Find the source. Who or what is judging your behavior?
- Separate yourself from that guilt source.
- Ask yourself, deep inside, what *you* believe, want, and choose for yourself.
- Correct the guilt producing behavior. Make amends.
- Listen to your self-talk. You talk yourself *into* feeling guilty; you can also talk yourself *out of* it.
- Forgive yourself and let it go.

Take time to examine your values and standards. Make a list of the rules in your childhood home. Evaluate them. Which do you want to keep? Which might you want to change? Once you begin to develop an "intrinsic conscience" based on your own values, beliefs, and choices, you will be released from general guilt. When you do something that *you* believe to be wrong, you will suffer *specific* guilt or regret that will help you to understand yourself better, serve to make you accountable, and lead you to better behavior next time.

Anger

*"Don't hold onto anger, hurt, or pain.
They steal energy and keep you from love."*

—Leo Buscaglia[8]

Eight-year-old Andy hits his little sister. His parent yells, "Stop that! Say you're sorry. Give her a big hug." Those orders ignore and deny Andy's feelings and demand hypocritical behavior; he's *not* sorry, and he doesn't feel like hugging her!

Here's another approach: Stop the behavior. ("You may not hit your sister!") Then realize that the behavior came from a feeling and a thought. He's hitting for a reason; he's probably angry. Accept his anger and help him *turn his feelings into words.* ("You're mad. What's going on?") Get into his shoes and understand what happened *from his point of view. Talking it out prevents acting it out.*

Channel the angry feelings into neutral or positive actions: "When you're angry, you can pound the pillows on your bed or hit the punching bag. You may *not* hit your sister." Andy concludes, "My feelings are okay. And I'm okay. It's not okay to hit my sister." He learns clear boundaries and some healthy ideas for dealing with his anger in the future.

In our culture, when little girls get mad, they quickly learn that it's not okay: nice girls don't get mad; it *is* okay to be hurt. On the other hand, when little boys get hurt, when a pet dies, for example, they quickly learn that boys don't cry. It's not okay to hurt; it is okay to get mad. For many people, emotions have been cross-wired. Women, when confronting someone in anger, may burst into tears; men suffering pain and loss may punch someone out. Yet anger, pain, joy and love are not male or female feelings; they are human emotions felt by everyone.

Anger is a normal feeling. It identifies a problem needing a solution. We must accept it in our children and in ourselves. When we learn to express it in a "clean," non-damaging way, it is easier to accept—in ourselves and in others.

If we were abused as children we had destructive, violent examples of how to be angry. We must now learn constructive ways to express anger so we don't end up hitting, exploding, or making ourselves sick by turning the anger inward.

A good thing to do when you're angry is to buy time. Say to your kids, "I'm feeling angry and I need to be alone for a few minutes so I don't take it out on you. We'll deal with it later." Then get away and do something to help you restore your reason—physical exercise, a shower, a phone call, a good cry, writing about it. Going off by yourself can give you a different perspective. Time out will help you regain your balance and enable you to deal with your children in a clean, non-damaging way, as well as model for them how to effectively deal with anger.

If the intensity of your anger is out of proportion to the situation, call a time-out to focus on what you "triggered." Get off by yourself so you can figure it out. Write about it in a notebook or journal. What happened? Why? What else was going on? What's underneath it? Once you unravel it, you defuse the trigger. One mother told her therapist that she "lost it" when her baby cried. Delving into this problem, they discovered that she had a belief that if her baby cried, it meant she was a "bad mother." Understanding this, she saw her error and changed her belief, her feelings, and her behavior.

Like other emotions, anger is usually short-lived. This is partly because it comes mixed with other feelings—fear, frustration, and love. Take, for example, the situation of a child getting lost in a store. Mother probably feels anger, fear, love, and relief when they are reunited; the common response, however, is to express only anger to the child. A healthier and more honest response would be to talk about the anger, then about the fear, the love—and the relief. Try this "Total Truth Process:"[9]

1. Express the anger: "I'm angry that you wandered off."
2. Express the pain and fear: "I was afraid that something bad might happen to you that would hurt you."
3. Express the "I'm sorrys": "I'm sorry that I was taking so long looking for shirts."
4. Express the wants: "What I want is for you to stay close enough to see me so I know you're okay. I want you to be safe and content. Maybe if I brought along some books or toys it would be more fun for you."
5. Express love, forgiveness, appreciation: "I am so glad that you are okay! I love you so much and don't want anything bad to happen to you." Hug and comfort the frightened child.

Many people get "stuck" in the anger, the pain, or the fear. Express one feeling, then move on until all the feelings are addressed and released. This is an amazing process. At first do this in letter form with no intention of sending it; this is for *you*—to release and heal your anger and pain. Start every section with "I". Try writing this "love letter" to get out of the anger and get back to the love. Once the negative feelings are released, the bottom line is, "I love you."

Other tools for dealing with anger include

- Deal with your anger as you'd like others to deal with theirs.
- Learn to release anger without harming self or others. *It is not okay to use emotional or physical violence.*
- Bite your tongue, if you have to, to avoid a cruel tirade.
- Keep it short, focusing on one problem only. Then forgive and forget.
- Separate the behavior from the person. Treat the person with respect and deal with the unacceptable behavior. Use "I-statements."
- Don't displace anger on an innocent person. It's not fair to make

your kids suffer because you're angry at your boss.
- Use active listening skills.
- Be honest. Kids can sense your feelings. But you don't have to tell them everything. You can say, "Sweetie, I'm angry right now, but I'm not angry at you. It's my problem and I'm working it out." Be truthful but not cruel.
- End on a positive note.
- If your anger is dangerous to you or others, get help.

Resentment

Unfinished business from the past has a way of reappearing. It nags at us demanding our attention and wanting a resolution. Anger and resentment possess us, punish us, and imprison us in the past. They create tension in our lives.

Pay attention to the tension, to the old nagging anger. Where does it come from? Whose voice do you hear? What did you do? Writing it out, follow it to its root cause.

One strategy for letting go of resentment is to write a letter to the person you resent. Take a moment to get in touch with all the feelings you still have concerning this person. Honestly allow those feelings to flow onto the paper without censoring them, because you really have no intention of mailing this letter. This one's for you. If the "old" pain reappears, write another letter. You may need to pound pillows, talk it out with a trusted friend, or find a therapist to help you deal with difficult emotions. The next and absolutely crucial step is to forgive yourself for having had "negative" feelings toward others and toward yourself.

Few parents intend to be cruel. Few people mean to be unfair. "If they don't mean it," you might ask, "why did they do it?" We may have been wounded in the past because:

- They may have thought that we deserved it. "This hurts me more than it hurts you," we heard as they inflicted punishment.
- They may have had poor impulse control. Drunk or enraged, they may have unfairly hurt us. They hadn't yet learned responsibility for their own feelings and behaviors.
- Their personal struggles may have spilled over onto the innocent. We may have been in the wrong place at the wrong time and been caught, for example, in the crossfire of a battle between Mom and Dad.
- They may have made mistakes and hurt us even though they had good intentions. They may have bungled or blundered while

trying to do their best. A depressed person—with intentions of lightening the burden of others—may, for example, take his life, creating a great deal of pain for his family.[10]

Resentment has a price. Pain denied and stuffed into the unconscious never loses its power; the wound does not heal. Our challenge is to face the pain squarely, to let go of the past and to move on with our lives. Forgiveness, of ourselves and others, dissolves the tension and releases old pain.

Forgiveness

People are not perfect. We have been hurt by mistakes of parents, teachers and other important adults in our lives. Blame and resentment trap us in the past—a past that is ancient history and has no place haunting and interfering with present life. Forgiveness releases us from that past and lets us heal ourselves and our memory. It sets us free from the prison of pain we never deserved. Forgiveness has a twofold purpose: to heal ourselves and to heal the damaged relationship.

The process begins with courage and a decision. It calls for willingness to be honest with yourself, to see more clearly and reframe your thinking. Unraveling faulty thinking can help us begin to heal. Many people overgeneralize: this is wrong; that is wrong; therefore, *everything* is wrong! They jump from a few specifics to a global catastrophe: "Everything's totally and completely awful."

To reverse this process, think of someone who is "all bad." Look for the specific behavior that bothers you; then consider all the other attributes that make up this person. What someone *does* is not who he or she *is*.

Separate who they are from what they did. When examining the pain, be very specific about the harmful incidents. What particular behavior wounded you?

Forgiveness does not mean approval. It involves a willingness to see with new eyes—to understand and to let go. They did what they did out of their own weakness. You did not deserve it. They could not teach you what they did not know. They could not give you what they did not have.

When you understand that they are not awful people but frail and needy persons who made painful mistakes, you are moving closer to forgiveness. When you can wish them well, you'll know that forgiveness has begun. As you peel off the layers of old hurt, anger, and guilt, underneath you'll discover a beautiful, lovable, more relaxed and

39

capable you.

In examining our old wounds, in releasing the anger and pain, we are insuring that we don't recreate the same wounds in those we love the most. We have all been wounded. Instead of wounding our children, let us heal ourselves.

> It doesn't matter your age, or your color,
> or whether your parents
> loved you or not
> (Maybe they wanted to, but couldn't.)
> Let that go.
> It belongs to the past.
> You belong to the NOW.
>
> It doesn't matter what you have been.
> The wrong you may have done.
> The mistakes you've made.
> The people you've hurt.
>
> You are forgiven.
> You are accepted.
> You are okay.
> You are loved—in spite of everything.
> So love yourself, and nourish the seed within you.
>
> Celebrate you.
> Begin NOW.
> Start anew.
> Give yourself a new birth today. . . .
> Today can be a new beginning, a new thing, a new life!
>
> —Clyde Reid[11]

Gratitude

We all have much to be thankful for. In visiting other countries, I notice many people who appear to be poor yet feel rich. In contrast, many Americans appear to be rich, yet feel poor. We don't appreciate how much we do have but instead are anxious about what we don't have.

High-powered television advertising, to which adults and children are subjected, instills in us a gnawing dissatisfaction with what we have and desire for what we don't have. Under its spell, we begin to think of our wants as needs. We are talked into *needing* items that we have survived without for many years. No matter how much we have, we are not satisfied; it's never enough. A Russian recently asked an American tourist, "Why do you need ten of everything?" In our culture we absolutely lust after material possessions.

The epidemic of perfectionism fuels the dissatisfaction. Perfectionists are always wanting something they don't have in order to fulfill their ideal image of being "perfect." This results in a future orientation that precludes deep satisfaction and is hard on true self-esteem.

Gratitude, on the other hand, reduces tension. Focusing on the positive aspects of ourselves, our children, and our parents lowers personal and interpersonal stress. Counting our blessings increases our joy.

We have much to be grateful for. My mother-in-law, Nida, although she lives meagerly, is grateful every morning simply that she has another day to enjoy, that the birds are singing, that there is food in the refrigerator. Noticing and giving thanks for the "little things" makes her life rich.

A friend of mine pauses before each meal to hold hands around the table with her family and guests and to give thanks—for the food, for each other, for whatever is positive in their lives. Rituals such as this are special times of closeness and appreciation.

With gratitude, we focus on what we do have, not on what we don't. Sprinkle your day with "thank yous". Everyone deserves more of them. Appreciation and recognition enhance self-esteem and make family living more fun.

"If the only prayer you say in your entire life is 'Thank you,' that would suffice."

—Meister Eckhart[12]

Emotions can be guides for making necessary and important choices in life. Expressing and accepting responsibility for our feelings is easier for people whose parents accepted their feelings when they were small.

If you have difficulty expressing your feelings, a very good friend, counselor, or support group could help you release the backlog and learn healthier ways to deal with your emotions. Don't keep them to yourself. Find a way to share them; take the risk. If you don't deal with them, they'll deal with you!

Ways to Cope[13]

When you are feeling:	And you're tempted to:	Choose a more helpful way to cope:
Nervous	Smoke	Make a list of your
Angry	Lose your temper	strengths
Lonely	Get in trouble	Get physical exercise
Wild	Overeat	Talk out your feelings
Disappointed	Turn to drugs	Take a walk
Bored	or alcohol	Do relaxation exercises
Tired	Stop eating	Ask for help
Down on yourself	Destroy something	Write a letter to a friend
Hurt	Make people angry	Do something that
Cheated	Drive too fast	makes you feel really
Discouraged	Spend money	good
	Worry so much you	Cook
	lose sleep	Make music
	Get in a fight	Dance
	Quit trying	Draw, paint
	Avoid the problem	Play sports
	Skip a meal	Clean a drawer or
	Give up	corner of your room
		Count to ten or a
		thousand
		Get involved
		Read
		Write out how you feel
		Plan something to look
		forward to
		Rest

8.

The Power of Words

"Healthy families remind each other of their goodness;
unhealthy families remind each other of their failings."

—Matthew Fox[1]

About twelve years ago while on a picnic in the mountains, my oldest son asked, "Mom, can I climb that mountain?" I gave him my okay; off he went. A little later my youngest son (about seven) asked, "Mom, can I climb that mountain?" "No, you're too clumsy," I responded without thinking. When I heard what I'd said, I wished I could eat my words, but it was too late.

Back home, Felix began to drop, spill, bump into, and fall over everything. He was probably saying to himself, "That important, all-knowing person who is my mother says that I'm clumsy; therefore I must be clumsy." It was a self-fulfilling prophecy. He became a walking disaster. Every time he went to pour milk, it was all over the counter. Knowing I was responsible for creating this monster, I was careful to not make an issue out of it; I simply encouraged him to clean it up. After about two weeks he finally returned to "normal." This experience was my initiation into understanding the power of words.

Since that time, I have learned how to undo clumsy words. I could have undone the harm by saying, "Felix, that was a clumsy thing I said, and I'm sorry," and given him a hug. Then I could have called Damian to take Felix with him up the mountain, or I might have climbed with him myself. Somehow I could have taken his request more seriously.

The language parents and teachers choose and the way they use it can determine a child's destiny. Words have the power to lift up or to put down. With our word choice we build or shred self-esteem.

The words that damage self-esteem are spoken without respect for others. They are spoken in a nasty tone of voice, and can be condescending or cruel. Sometimes as parents, when we feel we are not being heard, we "turn up the volume" in hopes of improving listening ability on the other end. More often than not, though, these strategies are counterproductive. They help turn people—especially kids—into losers. If your parents spoke to you this way, start listening to your own words and to the tone of your voice. Think about who it was that said those things to you. Remember how you felt hearing them and how those words shaped your behavior. Those old patterns may still be operating in your life.

Fortunately, once you have awareness, you have a choice. You can choose to "go on automatic," to do to your kids what was done to you (even though you hated it), or you can choose to become the kind of parent you would like to have had. You can react knee-jerk fashion and put your kids down and probably regret it later. Or you can choose to respond, instead, with care and wisdom.

When you next catch yourself about to react, take three deep belly-breaths and some time out. Pause to evaluate your thoughts and feelings, and the consequences of possible actions. Think of the positive outcome you want to accomplish and how to bring that about. When you respond, others tend to listen and cooperate. When you react, others tend also to react.

Listen to the words coming out of your mouth. What effect do they have on others? What effect do they have on you? Do you really want to do/say those things?

Many times we need to bite our tongues to stop a nasty statement from slipping out. In fact, a bit of scar tissue on the tip of the tongue could be a badge of honor. It means we cared enough to stop, take time to cool off, and then to talk about the problem later when we could tell the kids what we were feeling and what we wanted.

Living in a family requires us to interact with and respond to others. We can do this negatively with criticism or positively with feedback.

Self-Esteem Shredders

Killer statements are most damaging. They should never be used. Examples are

- "Don't be you."
- "You were a mistake."
- "I wish you had been a boy."
- "I wish you had never been born."
- "If I didn't have you, I could have a career."

Behaviors that convey the same damaging messages are constant ignoring, rejection, battering/abuse, and acting or speaking as if the child were not there when he or she is there. Killer statements are deadly—psychologically and physically. Don't ever use them.

Crooked communication refers to statements that sound positive at first but that have a negative, damaging twist (left-handed compliments). I think of the greeting cards that look cute and funny on the outside yet are cutting and hurtful on the inside. The statements are often sarcastic, insincere, or patronizing.

- "You're pretty good at math—for a girl."
- "Oh, you *never* make a mistake."
- "You *always* know the answer, don't you, smarty pants?"

Crooked communication is confusing and painful; it erodes self-esteem.

Negative ways of dealing with negative behavior[2] include criticism, put-downs, ridicule, name calling, blaming, and rejection. "You-statements" are common ("You can't do anything right." "What's wrong with you?" "How could you be so stupid?" "You always get into trouble." "When are you going to grow up?"). They are usually delivered in a nasty tone of voice and are often exaggerated ("You always_____" or "you never_____"). Related to external force (and punishment), you-statements attack all of you, your whole person. Focusing on what they don't want, they don't communicate what they *do* want.

Many of us were raised on you-statements. Take a moment and return to your childhood. Remember times when people spoke to you that way. What did they say to you? How did they say it? What did you feel about yourself? About them? What conclusions did you draw? How did those incidents affect your relationship with the other person(s) involved?

You-statements mostly feel like attacks, and when we feel attacked we want to protect and defend ourselves and tune out those painful words. We cannot understand how the people who claim to love us can hurt us this way. Instead of being able to respond appropriately, we lock into fear and self-protection, compliance or defiance.

The intent of the parent—to deal with and change behavior—is honorable. The negative methods used to achieve it don't work. You-statements don't teach children what it is that you *do* want. Mostly parents don't talk about that. Instead, they teach fear. Children hear you and conclude, "I'm no good." "I can't do anything right." "I'm worthless." "I'm not lovable." "I can't trust you." "You don't care about me." The criticism—the emotional abuse—leads to anger, withdrawal, and rejection. The self-esteem of both parent and child is damaged, and the relationship between the two may be harmed.

It should be noted that not all you-statements are damaging; for example, "You did a good job!" "You need to finish putting away the dishes," or "You must be proud of yourself." The tone of voice will usually let them know.

If you were brought up hearing negative messages, you have probably caught yourself saying things to your children that you swore you never would say. It is hard to change behavior, especially habitual ways of acting and speaking, but it can be done. It begins with awareness, then a commitment, then working at it. The payoff for you and your children will be tremendous.

Many destructive patterns keep repeating themselves simply because we don't know of better ways to deal with problems. It is crucial that we expand our options. In the days when extended families were the rule and not the exception, there were many role models. We could see how Uncle John played with his kids and how Aunt Judy solved problems with hers. Today, with smaller families, we may be unaware of many options available to us because we have never seen them. Let us now discuss some of the positive options that are open to us.

Self-Esteem Builders

Words that build self-esteem are spoken with respect for the other person and with caring about what is going on inside. They are encouraging, and they invite people to become winners. The tone of voice is "clean," not charged with negative emotion. A loving touch—a pat on the back, a hug—often accompanies the words. This is positive feedback.

Positive strokes for being are nourishing and life-giving.[3] Feedback can "feed" the spirit, validate others, and make them want to be winners. Read the following statements and be aware of what feelings they evoke in you.

- "You are special and unique."
- "You are important to me."
- "I like you!"
- "I love you."
- "I believe in you."
- "I'm glad you're here."

Nonverbally these are expressed by an attitude of respect and enjoyment, by affection, by taking the children seriously, by spending time with them, and by really listening.

Rewards for doing recognize effort or improvement and show appreciation. Feedback encourages children to do things well.

- "Fantastic!"
- "Atta boy!"
- "It looks like you did your best on that."
- "Keep up the good work."

- "Go ahead—try it."
- "Look at the progress you've made." (See Appendix B.)

Too many children, too many husbands and wives feel unappreciated. Frequent "Thank yous" and pats on the back sweeten life and prevent burnout. Give positive strokes not only for accomplishments but also for effort: "Thanks for trying." Everyone needs more appreciation than they're getting. Turn this around. Give others—and yourself— more appreciation than you think is needed. Watch how things change.

Many kids and adults have difficulty with compliments, so they flip one back ("I like yours, too") or shrug it off ("This old thing?"). They don't know what to do with them. It's really very simple: someone has given you a gift, so just say thank you. If you trust their sincerity, all you have to do is take a deep breath and let it in.

Compliments, like feedback, are more effective when they are descriptive and specific. "I like how you help your brother" gives more useful information than "You're such a wonderful boy." (Hearing you're wonderful can, however, be very nourishing.)

Positive ways of dealing with negative behavior should be given with respect and caring. It is important to deal with unacceptable behavior. We do this by giving them feedback about inappropriate behavior. It's equally important to support and encourage positive behavior and to invite children to become winners.

The underlying message behind feedback is acceptance, valuing, and inspiring the other to be better. It is a strategy for changing others through guidance, encouragement, and support. Feedback is given as a gift to another out of caring. It is given as a suggestion—something important for the other to consider—rather than an order. It works by motivating the other to be good, by creating a desire in the other person to correct the situation.

As parents we must set reasonable and healthy limits for our children. The most effective way for us to deal with inappropriate behavior is to *separate the behavior from the person*. They are okay, their behavior is not; we love them, but we do not like what they did.

"I-statements" are an effective way of dealing with undesirable behavior. The model is: "I feel _____ when you _____ because _____, and what I want is _____." ("I feel mad when you leave your shoes on the living-room floor because they make the room look messy, and what I want is for you to put them under your bed.") I-statements are specific, keeping the focus on the behavior, not on the person. They clearly state what it is that you *do* want. With I-statements, children learn cause and effect relationships (Mom feels _____ because I did _____), and they learn judgment skills.[4]

Another way to deal with negative behavior is with *substitution*. Stop the behavior you don't want; then encourage the behavior you do want. For example, "Don't do _____. Do _____ instead." ("Don't hit your sister, hit a pillow or your punching bag instead.") Another approach is "Don't do _____. You can figure out a better way to do it." Every parent has taken a dangerous object from a toddler and replaced it with a toy. With substitution, we stop the undesirable behavior and lead the child to more acceptable behavior.

Feedback, well given, feels like a gift. There is no need for defensiveness. The child observes the acceptance, respect, and caring and concludes, "Mom/ Dad cares about me enough to tell me this and encourage me to be better. I am important. I am worthwhile." The self-esteem of both parties is enhanced. The language and approach allow the receiver to hear what is being said, and the desired change in behavior is more likely to happen.

Observe these two models of critical vs. helpful means of response:

	CRITICISM	FEEDBACK
Leadership Style:	Autocratic. Respect may be lacking. Little concern for self-esteem.	Democratic. Based on respect for others, concern about the relationship and maintaining self-esteem.
Based on:	External pressure or force.	Internal motivation.
Underlying message:	You must do things *my way*.	I accept and value you, and encourage you to do better.
Language:	You-statements which may be global. "This is how you are."	I-statements which are descriptive, specific, and limited to the issue at hand.
Strategies:	Focuses on the person. The whole person is labeled, putdown, rejected. Orders and manipulates. Interactions charged with emotion.	Focuses on behavior. Gives specific information based on personal experience, delivered in a matter-of-fact, friendly, or stern matter.
Response of other:	Feels like an attack; it arouses fear & self-protection, compliance or defiance.	Well delivered, it feels like a gift.

Time frame:	Focuses on the past, even drawing in situations from years ago.	Deals with the present; focuses on the future ("And next time I want ___.")
Outcomes:	Disempowerment, damaged relationship, low self-esteem.	Empowerment, enhanced relationship, high self-esteem.

The "hook" with criticism is that it goes on after they go off.[5] It gets inside and repeats like a broken record. If you pause and listen to your own negative self-talk, you may be able to identify the voices of the important people who, years ago, criticized you ("You're bad." "You're stupid." "You can't do anything right!") The negative self-talk process can be interrupted and corrected. (See Chapter 16.)

Once you decide to use a better way, you need to break old habits. "Turn-about statements" can help you do that. Some people say: "That's the way I am", or "I can't help it if I'm____," or "I'm the kind of person who____." Those phrases keep them stuck in the past. Instead say, "I used to criticize my kids a lot, but now I'm learning to give them feedback instead"; or, "In the past I____, but now____." Such turn-about statements can help the transition between how you used to be and who you are becoming.

When you hear negative words slip out, you can also stop yourself and say something like: "I'm sorry! I didn't want to say that. Let me say it over." You can talk it over with your kids or spouse and ask them to remind you when you slip, by saying perhaps, "Replay, Mom," or "Ouch, dad, try again." or giving another signal. It is possible to change behaviors. It's a bit easier with support and encouragement from others and from yourself.

Halting criticism is an extremely important step to building self-esteem. Equally important is increasing the number of positive strokes—appreciation, compliments, and support. As we decrease the negative attention and increase the positive, we increase satisfaction and joy for the whole family.

9.

Parenting Responses That Affect Self-Esteem

"Every time I get in trouble you remind me of everything I've ever done wrong in my life. I'm not too sure what kind of person I am, but you're convincing me I'm bad."

—A junior high school student[1]

For better or worse, adults constantly influence the self-esteem of children—whether they realize it or not—whether they intend it or not. The words they use fall into four basic types of responses: Nurturing and Structuring Responses which increase self-esteem, and Marshmallowing and Criticizing Responses, which tear it down.[2] Read these examples, noticing how they feel to you.

Situation 1

Twelve-year-old Annie says, "I want to sleep at Janet's tonight. Her parents won't be there, but her sixteen-year-old brother will."

Nurturing Response: "You'd like to have fun with your friend tonight. Invite her to come here for the night."

Structuring Response: "No. Unless her parents are home, you may not spend the night there."

Marshmallowing Response: "Well, I don't like the idea, but I guess just this one time wouldn't hurt."

Criticizing Response: "No! Of course not! What would people think of us? And don't you know what sixteen-year-old boys are after?"

Situation 2

Judith says, "My husband is away on business, and the baby is driving me up the wall."

Nurturing Response: "You're in a difficult situation, Judith. Ask for help—you need it. And the baby needs a mother who is not up the wall. You'll both be better off when you start taking care of yourself."

Structuring Response: "Call someone for help. Find a church or agency that offers child care. Take care of yourself and your baby."

Marshmallowing Response: "Poor thing. There just isn't any good help available these days. I hope you make it."

Criticizing Response: "If you were a better mother, you wouldn't have that problem!"

Situation 3

Eight-year-old Ryan won't clean his room and says, "I hate you, Mom."

Nurturing Response: "Ryan [touching him], I know you don't want to clean your room and that you're mad at me. That's okay. I still love you. Let's both clean our rooms at the same time, and when we finish, we'll go outside and play."

Structuring Response: "We're all part of the family, Ryan, and we all have chores to do. Cleaning your room is an important way of being part of our team."

Marshmallowing Response: "Don't hate me. You're right, it is too hard for you. I'll do it for you so we can be pals. Maybe when you get bigger you'll be able to do something by yourself, poor thing."

Criticizing Response: "You bad boy! Get in your room right now and don't come out until it's perfect! And just wait 'til your father gets home!"

Nurturing Responses

Based on respect, love and support, nurturing responses encourage self-responsibility. Parents invite children to get their needs met and offer help in doing so. They believe their kids are winners with the capacity to grow; they give them permission to succeed. I-statements and affectionate touch are used.

Structuring Responses

Also based on respect, structuring responses protect, set limits, and demand performance ("I know you can do it!"). Parents expect and encourage children to be capable and responsible. They encourage them to ask for what they need and want, thereby empowering them.

Nurturing and structuring responses fit together nicely. The underlying message for both is, "You are a valuable resource who can be even better. I encourage and promote your growth." The use of these messages results in cooperation, empowerment, win-win situations, and high self-esteem.

Marshmallowing Responses

Based on judging children to be weak and inadequate, marshmallowing responses disempower while sounding supportive. Blaming other persons, the situation, or fate for the problem, they remove responsibility from the child, inviting dependence and encouraging failure. You statements are commonly used: "Why don't you quit." "You poor thing, there's nothing you can do." "I'll do it for you."

Criticizing Responses

Based on disrespect, criticizing responses encourage children to fail. Ridicule, put-downs, blaming, fault-finding, comparing, and labeling are common. You-statements are often global: "You always ____". "You never ____". Humor is cruel; touch is hurtful or punishing. Marshmallowing and criticizing responses are damaging to self-esteem. They result in anger and resentment, in passivity, dependence, and powerlessness.

Which response styles did your parents mostly use? Are you glad they treated you that way? Which style do you mostly use? How do you feel about treating your children that way?

Many parents find themselves doing to their kids what they swore they'd never do—then feel guilty about it. It is possible to change your style! And when you let go of the handed-down damaging behavior, your self-esteem will go up, and so will everyone else's. It's not easy to change habits *but you can do it if you really want to!* You will thank yourself a thousand times over; so will your children—and your grandchildren.

One mom yelled at her son, "I'm going to beat you!" Then she stopped herself realizing that she didn't *want* to beat him and added "... with a sock...with your dad's smelly sock!" She beamed with pride telling her story. Later she wrote me a letter: "I'm really excited with the changes in our lives. I really AM becoming the parent I wish I'd had."

Here are some specific strategies for changing from negative to positive response styles.

• **Change your focus**. Instead of always catching your kids being "bad," catch them being good: what you look for, you find. Once you

look for the things they're doing right, you'll be surprised at what neat kids they are. Give them lots of encouragement and support ("Good for you!") for positive behavior.

We all need "strokes." People prefer to get positive strokes, but they'd rather get negative strokes than nothing at all (being ignored). So focus on and encourage the qualities and behaviors you do want.

• **Expect the best.** Kids want to live up to our expectations—unless those expectations are unrealistic or impossible. Expectations of perfection lead to disappointment and despair. Marshmallowing and criticizing parents expect the worst—and they get it! Nurturing and structuring parents expect the best—and they get it!

Do you believe that kids are worthless and a bother? If so, you will expect that, look for that, and get that. If, on the other hand, you believe that kids are valuable resources who can become even better, you will expect, look for, and get that.

• **Give up blaming and fault-finding.** Criticizing parents look for what's wrong, find it, then put down the other person in order to feel one-up and superior. But no one likes to be put down, ridiculed, humiliated, or blamed. Criticism leads to resentment and anger—or passivity and dependency. It results in powerlessness and discouragement. Everyone's self-esteem suffers.

Nurturing and structuring parents avoid blaming and fault-finding; they think, instead, in terms of responsibility. Responsibility means "the ability to respond." Everyone is encouraged to assume responsibility for his or her behaviors and their consequences. When a mistake is made, it's not the end of the world—it just needs to be fixed. It's easier for children to assume responsibility when they understand that mistakes are opportunities for learning, not for ridicule and shame.

One fall, when I was working on the tomato harvest, I found a broken canning jar in the kitchen. I could have yelled and blamed someone. Instead I asked who knew about the jar. I needed to be sure there was no broken glass to cut bare feet. In questioning my children I found out that it was broken when my son removed it from the dishwasher; somehow he hadn't noticed. So together we checked out the machine and removed all the remaining broken glass. We both responded to the situation (assumed responsibility for it) and resolved the problem without anyone's self-esteem being damaged.

As parents, we are needed to provide structure, not criticism, and if we pay attention, we see the results of our parenting responses every day. If we make a commitment to ourselves and to our children to make our responses nurturing and growth-producing, they in turn will respond to us by being better, more responsible people—with higher self-esteem.

10.

Parents Are Leaders: Re-Visioning Your Family

"Better one word before than two after."

—Welsh Proverb

Maybe no one told you this, but as a parent, you are a king, a queen, a president. You are an important leader with tremendous power. With this power you can create health, happiness, and high self-esteem in your family, building strong, caring citizens out of your children.

There are five basic components to leadership. Using the example of leading a horse, they come more clear:

• **Vision/direction/goals.** In leading a horse, I must know where I am going—to the barn. Success is more likely if I consider the needs of the horse. If he's very thirsty, I can almost count on having a power struggle unless I allow him to get a drink as we pass the water tank. Once he gets a drink, we can continue to the barn. When we are sensitive to and respectful of others' needs, we can usually both come out winning.

• **Focus on what I want.** It's important to keep sight of my vision—the barn. I need to focus on what I *do* want, not on what I don't want.

• **Communicate the message.** I must let the horse know what I want and head it toward the barn. Parents are teachers who must clearly communicate to their children what it is they want.

• **Support the desired progress.** As the horse moves in the desired direction, I encourage and support his progress toward the barn. Likewise with children. We don't wait until a toddler speaks clearly in complete sentences to cheer; we get excited about each understandable word and phrase.

• **Expect success and get it.** I fully expect that we will get to the barn, and we will. Your expectations that your children are healthy and responsible will nudge them on that path.

These components describe *proactive leadership*. Proactive leadership sets out what is wanted in advance and leads the way to it. Most of life's problems can be anticipated and avoided. Proactive leadership (also known as prevention) takes the children away from trouble and danger and redirects them to a better, safer activity.

The more common style of leadership is *reactive*. Reactive leadership may seem easier to do (if it has become habitual), yet it actually creates more difficulty and stress. Many parents don't know what they *do* want for their children, and therefore they don't tell them. The unsuspecting child innocently does something and gets jumped on: "You shouldn't have done that!" The kid is confused and angry because nobody ever told him or her not to do it.

Example: Molly walks past some toys on the bottom stair; Mom reacts by yelling, "Why didn't you take those upstairs?" The answer is that Molly wasn't told and she's not a mind-reader; but of course she doesn't say that. Both parties are angry, and Molly is confused. Anxiety and fear are a way of life.

Reactive parents frequently resort to threats, force, criticism, humiliation, ridicule, and punishment which create negative feelings both in their children and themselves. Self-esteem plunges. With a little foresight, this is usually preventable. Parents must clearly communicate what they want in advance. It makes life much easier.

Examples of Leadership Styles

Proactive Leadership	Reactive Leadership
• "childproofs" a home as baby begins to toddle	• changes nothing and constantly says no
• removes broken glass from the yard before a foot is cut	• removes broken glass from the foot
• lets a child know that you must leave in 15 minutes, then perhaps sets a timer for 10 minutes	• waits until it's time to leave, then gets angry because the child is not ready
• tells children you're going to a restaurant and explains desired behavior	• takes unprepared children to a restaurant, then threatens never to take them again
• says, to teen "I hope you'll always let me know where you are and when you'll be back; call if you're late"	• does not discuss plans and expectations in advance, then yells at the teen when she gets home late

Proactive leadership identifies dangers lurking in the world and gives kids permission, encouragement, and support to resist the pressures. I remember Felix commenting that all the billboards in the city were advertising alcohol. I pointed out emphatically how advertising links drugs and alcohol with fun, success, and beauty; we are all being manipulated to want to use pain killers, sleeping pills, and other drugs as a way of life. He later entered the "party scene" years with open eyes, and never felt compelled to take stupid risks with substances.

The Language of Leadership

Proactive Leadership
(looks toward the future)

Reactive Leadership
(focuses on the past)

• "That was awful. I know you can do better."	• "Why did you ___?"
	• "Why didn't you ___?"
• "Next time I want you to ___."	• "You shouldn't have ___ ."
• "Why don't you try ___."	

Reactive leaders reinforce unwanted behavior by focusing on the past which we can not change. Proactive leaders deal with present inappropriate behavior, then lead the child toward improving. ("How can you do it better next time?") They give another chance while guiding and encouraging progress toward the desired behavior. An ounce of foresight is worth a pound of hindsight.

Think, for a moment about the leadership style of your parents. Was it proactive or reactive? How was it for you? How did it affect your self- esteem? What do you want for your children?

Re-Visioning Your Family

When in council, Iroquois Indians have a long-range vision. They consider whether their decisions will benefit their people for the next seven generations. Their vision guides their daily actions and their lives.

Vision, direction, and goals are the basis of good leadership. What vision have you for your family in five years? In ten years? In twenty years? In what ways do you want your family to be like the family of your childhood? How do you want it to be different? You have the power not only to create a vision but to live it.

In re-visioning our families, we are led to examine our values. What were the important qualities of the family of your childhood? What was valued? Note which of the following characteristics apply to you.

performance • perfection • work • being "good" • possessions
being who you are • adventure • conformity • trust • authority
avoiding conflict • a clean house • friendships • travel
spontaneity • rules • fun • love • choices • acceptance
being obedient • thinking for yourself • openness and honesty
being pretty and clean • being "nice" • being religious •
connectedness • integrity • family unity • taking care of yourself
safety • pleasing others • isolation • keeping down the pain • play
respect • responsibility • self-protection • encouragement
discouragement • risking • taking care of others • belonging

Which of these characteristics led to health and happiness for you and your brothers and sisters? Which did not? Which do you now choose for your own family? Keep the vision broad (not "I want my son or daughter to be a doctor"), focusing on qualities and values—not specific goals—that will enhance your lives. Knowing what you want is the first step in getting it.

Many years ago I had an important insight. I realized that if I trusted outside voices more than my inner voice, when values clashed, I would be teaching my children values that I didn't believe in and create confusion and conflict. (See Chapter 21.) Specifically, I believe that force and violence are wrong, yet my children were learning from many sources that violence was an accepted way to get what they wanted. I realized that it was important to reexamine and clarify all my values, to pass on those that I truly believed in and discard those that were not really meaningful to me.

Examine your values. What is your personal code of ethics? We must teach our children right from wrong. They need basic values and manners in order to get along with others. Teach kindness, respect, and honesty. Teach them the Golden Rule: *Do unto others as you would have others do unto you.* What we model is what we teach best —and what our children tend to become.

Once you have your own vision of a Winning Family, take a small step every day in that direction. Believe in your vision, then communicate it. This can be done in many ways. For example, when my daughter was small, I said to her, "One day you'll be a beautiful, strong woman." To my sons I said, "Someday you'll grow up to be wonderful, gentle men." Without realizing it at the time, I was planting seeds of my vision in my children. Now, as adults, each is sensitive and each is strong.

Talk about your vision. Encourage and listen to their visions. ("If I could give the world the best present, I'd give....") Then inspire, encourage and support them. Celebrate the little steps of progress.

A leader is best
When people barely know that he exists,
Not so good when people obey and acclaim him,
Worst when they despise him.
"Fail to honor people,
They fail to honor you."
But of a good leader, who talks little,
When his work is done, his aim fulfilled,
They will all say, "We did this ourselves."

—Lao Tzu

11.

Parenting Leadership Styles

*"To revere power above everything else
is to be willing to sacrifice everything else to power."*

—Marilyn French [1]

Were you raised by tyrants? If your home politics were so rigid that the strict rules were not balanced with flexibility and freedom, your parents employed an autocratic leadership style—keeping and over-using power. Were you raised by not being raised? Was there too much freedom and flexibility with no rules for behavior, and little guidance when you needed it? If so, your parents were permissive; they relinquished their power or didn't know they had it. Or were you raised by leaders who balanced their power with freedom, and caring? If so, your parents shared power in a democratic leadership style. The leadership style parents use reflects their self-esteem and affects the personality and self-esteem of their children.

Most	Control/Structure/Guidance	Least
←		→
Autocratic	Democratic	Permissive

These styles reflect different uses of power and control—from over-powering at the left to abdicating at the right.

Love is the other dimension of parenting. Love enhances each leadership style, making it healthier for the family. Add love to the autocratic style, and it becomes more caring and less damaging. The permissive style without love and support is neglect. Love is the baseline for mental health and successful family life.

After you've identified your parents' leadership style, reflect on how it affected you. Did you like it? Was it good for you? What kind of a relationship do you now have with your parents? Is that what you want to have with your children when they grow up?

Often, children who dislike their parents' style vow that they will bring up their own children differently. Many swing from one extreme to the other, creating a new family perhaps with as many problems, only different ones. This swing is commonly from the autocratic to the permissive style.

Autocratic Leadership Style

Characteristics of Parents

Autocratic or "drill sergeant" parents impose their will through a rigid structure of rules, allowing little flexibility or freedom. They tend to

- overuse or abuse power
- impose their will through rigid rules
- take total control and responsibility for all decisions
- take charge of other people's lives
- think that their way is the only right way
- withhold information
- be out of touch with their feelings (or shut them down)
- ignore or put down the opinions and feelings of others; e.g., "You're too sensitive".
- use pressure and punishment to force compliance
- hurt others

Autocratic parents demand "respect", which sometimes translates as "fear". They may believe that children should be seen and not heard, and that a child's will must be broken.

Feelings of Parents

Autocratic parents generally feel

- superior (one-up) and in control
- distrust (or lack trust)
- burdened with responsibility
- lonely
- low-self-esteem

Feelings of Children

In this type of family configuration, children will tend to feel

- powerless and out of control
- submissive and dependent, or hostile and angry

- distrusting, helpless
- self-rejecting
- lonely, with low self-esteem

These children feel afraid and guilty, yet they don't know what to do with their feelings since they are ignored or denied by their parents.

Characteristics of Children

Placed in a one-down, inferior position to their parents (even when grown), these children work hard at second-guessing, trying to figure out how to *please* their parents and avoid getting punished. They

- want to be told what to do
- lack a sense of personal responsibility
- may distrust their feelings because they've been told those feelings are "wrong"
- become self-rejecting and lonely
- are compliant and withdrawing (accepting powerlessness) or defiant and rebellious (fighting for power)
- may withdraw by moving or running away

One young mother reported that she had rebelled against her autocratic parents by getting pregnant and keeping her baby in spite of the fact that they wanted her to have an abortion. Another woman got back at her father by marrying the "wrong" man. An older woman had dealt with her autocratic parents by moving to Japan. Adolescents who feel out of control of their lives may develop eating disorders to assert control over their own bodies. The autocratic leadership style may work for a period of time, but tends to break down when children become teenagers.

Permissive Leadership Style

Characteristics of Parents

In the very permissive family, there is *too much* freedom. Parents abdicate power, and there are often no rules, limits, or structure. If rules do exist, they are always changing, which results in chaos. Permissive parents tend to

- believe they have no rights
- condone everything their children do

- not be interested in their children or what they do
- be physically or emotionally absent and uninvolved
- neglect their children

Feelings of Parents

These parents often feel

- discouraged
- confused and angry
- powerless and out of control over their lives
- disrespected
- overwhelmed
- low self-esteem

Feelings of Children

Children in these families often feel

- powerless and out of control
- unsafe
- unloved
- confused and discouraged
- dependent
- unable to cope with routine
- low self-esteem

Surrounded by confusion and inconsistency, these children don't feel they can trust their parents.

Characteristics of Children

In permissive families, children

- have trouble with limits (while at the same time craving them)
- lack self-discipline and responsibility (or may have had to assume too much responsibility too soon)
- may take on the unhealthy role reversal with parents
- are often on their own before they are ready
- think they have the right to do exactly as they wish
- have little awareness of social responsibility
- may become violent toward thier parents
- may later seek out highly structured groups, cults, institutions

Democratic Leadership Styles

Characteristics of Parents

Democratic families are based on respect. *Everyone's* needs are considered important. Parents share power with each other and with their children. They offer choices and treat children as capable, worthwhile human beings who are able to think for themselves and make good decisions. They teach responsibility and allow freedom. There may be family meetings involving everyone in making decisions, rules, and plans. There is a balance of power between husband and wife; neither is solely "the boss." Democratic parents

- give their children choices appropriate to their ages, and let them learn from the consequences
- provide structure while allowing flexibility and freedom
- invite and encourage children to participate in planning and decision making, yet enforce the rules
- teach responsibility by giving it
- encourage children to learn from mistakes and fix them

Democratic parents function as counselors and coaches. This style—when based on love—is the framework for a winning family.

Feelings of Parents

Democratic parents start from an attitude of cooperation with their children. They

- are in charge, yet flexible
- feel respectful and respected, loving and loved
- trust their children and themselves
- are sensitive to needs
- have high self-esteem

Feelings of Children

In democratic families, children know they are responsible for themselves and their behavior. They feel

- trusted and respected
- worthwhile and important
- self-confident and self-respecting

They have a high level of self-esteem and a sense of personal power.

Characteristics of Children

Having a team sense, these children are eager to cooperate. They

- respect rules
- are self-disciplined and responsible
- understand cause-effect relationships
- are capable and self-determining

Through making choices and decisions, children of democratic families learn to direct their own lives. They have a friendly relationship with their parents that can someday become a mutual relationship between equals. (See Appendix C.)

A husband and wife attending my workshop came to the realization that *he* was authoritarian and *she* was permissive. The more he swung one way, the more she swung the other. This was confusing to their children and difficult for the whole family. With this insight into their conflict, this couple had an opportunity to make new choices.

A teenage girl talked about life in her autocratic family: "Often it gets to the point where home seems like a concentration camp, and it becomes a challenge to 'escape.' Tension builds to a disastrous point, with too much emphasis put on chores. People start fighting and hurting each other." She continued in a letter to her parents, "Don't make chores the most critical and important factor in the household. Don't judge kids on their ability or concern about chores. Coach and help them without exerting power and forcing them to buckle under your iron will. Try to understand each child's needs, other obligations, physical capabilities, attention span, and allow reasonable leeway for these considerations.

"If anger should arise, restrain yourself, and under no circumstances call your children names as you have done in the past. Children and teenagers are highly susceptible to labels: if you call him incompetent, he *thinks* he is, and therefore *becomes* incompetent. If you call him stupid, lazy, slow, useless, clumsy, or irresponsible, he is. He can be devastated by one careless word thrown in anger. Avoid that anger, and keep your children feeling worthy and confident, making each chore simply a duty rather than a futile struggle."

In our democratic society, where people must be able to make decisions, think for themselves, and vote for their leaders, the democratic family is the foundation for the skills, for responsibility and for a sense of teamwork. As parents, we are not actually building "cathedrals"—rather, we are supplying our children with the best quality materials available so they can design and build them themselves.

The autocratic family was the only style that I knew, and therefore it was the style that I "naturally" employed with my young family. As they grew and became able to think, communicate, and be more responsible, I found that I could "loosen up." I gradually let go of my need to be in control, and they were ready and willing to assume more control and responsibility for themselves. As I trusted them more, they became more trustworthy; as they became more trustworthy, I trusted them more. Shifting from external control to motivation from within, I gradually evolved into a democratic leadership style. We were becoming a team. In retrospect, I see that what I did is in harmony with the second basic dimension of a healthy family. When children are little, we have complete responsibility for their care and protection. As they grow and develop, we can gradually turn over or share the power and responsibility with them.

Democratic parents share power with their children, creating a relationship based on mutual empowerment—instead of mutual victimization. As we teach children that they can choose to be who they want to be and do what they want to do with their lives, we are empowering them. This empowerment is necessary for mental health, for making dreams come true, and for self-esteem in your children and yourself.

12.

Parenting and Empowerment

"When you give away some of the light from the candle
by lighting another person's candle,
there isn't less light because you've given some away—there's more.
When everybody grows, there isn't less of anybody,
there's more of—and for—everybody."

—Kaleel Jamison[1]

Healthy parenting is nothing if not a process of empowerment. As we help to raise our children's self-esteem, we also increase their personal power. When we encourage them to be confident, self-reliant, self-directed, and responsible individuals, we are giving them power. For better or worse, the patterns of power by which we live, and which we model, will profoundly affect their entire lives. And as parents, we have much to gain by learning to share power with our children.

As a mom I taught and encouraged my kids to ride bicycles. There was a rush of pride and power—and a tinge of surprise—as they'd yell back to me: "I'm doing it!" Nearly twenty years after I'd given my oldest son, Damian, one last push on his wobbly two-wheeler, he spent an afternoon looking for the "perfect" bike for me. He taught and encouraged me to use it, giving me that same push back! The icing on the cake came when the whole family had the chance to go touring in Europe—me on my special bike! Each of us was able to push our own pedals and pull our own weight for many days and zillions of kilometers (or so it seemed). It was a satisfying and empowering experience for each and every one of us.

My youngest son, Felix, has taught me things I would never have learned on my own. When I'd ask him to fix something for me, he'd show me how to do it. Under his guidance, I've become a veritable whiz on a computer. In discussing my own process of empowerment with him, he laughed, "Yeah, Mom, we had a wimp rehabilitation program for you;" again, the power I gave my son came back to me. And over the years, I've raised my daughter, Kristen, to believe in herself

71

and in her artistic talent. Now she is proving it to me, empowering my own career and book with many forms of her expression. As a mom, I encouraged my kids to use their personal power. Now I know that they have the power to live healthy and effective lives.

When I was a child myself, however, I was told and thus believed that my purpose in life was to be a nice little girl. When I grew up, I found I was a very nice lady. By being "nice" I avoided situations that called for much power and yielded to others to avoid power struggles. I was acutely aware of my isolation and lack of support and had little sense of my own personal power.

My children, however, taught me differently. Through the conflict-ridden process of being a mother and "just a housewife", I became aware of an awesome power and responsibility: to give life, to nurture, and to shape young beliefs and behaviors.

When I studied psychology in graduate school, I began to recognize a common thread through my courses and my own experience. Everyone needs to feel confident, to feel competent, to have a sense of power. I spent the next twelve years or so unravelling the fabric of my own beliefs and behaviors, and letting go of those that held me back. Bit by bit, I began to re-weave the pieces. The new attitudes, skills, and habits have formed a cloak of power that is all my own.

Power comes from the Latin word *poder*, meaning "to be able." Everyone needs to be able, to be capable, to have a sense of personal power. At the heart of personal power is the knowledge that you are in charge of your life—that you have the ultimate responsibility for how you live it. In accepting more and more responsibility for your own self and your behavior, you gain personal power. In connecting and collaborating with others, you expand that power.

Power comes in many forms. There is talk about buying power, staying power, power lunches, political power, power dressing, and a thing called "clout". Certain roles—president, principal, policeman, and parent—have power inherent in the job description. Success, in this country, is commonly measured by power in the form of money, status, and/or control and influence over others. With this kind of thinking, power is a pie and there are not enough slices to go around.

Power Associations

Power means different things to different people. Some positive associations include:

- having choices
- making a difference
- being able to bring about change

- influencing others
- responsibility
- expressing one's uniqueness.

Such associations make people desire power. (You can think of more.)

Yet sometimes the word makes people nervous because of the many negative associations:

- domination and oppression
- violence and abuse
- patriarchy and sexism
- rape and incest
- racism and slavery
- militarism and war
- manipulation, exploitation, and seduction
- dishonesty and secrets
- a burdensome responsibility for others

Power can be intoxicating and lead people to do inhumane things to others; power can corrupt. It can also destroy lives.

Power Games

Many kids these days play video games where you either explode something or get exploded; they learn that in order for one person to win, the other has to lose. The concept, "I want you to lose so that I can win," is deeply woven into the fabric of how we think and who we are. Unfortunately, this up/down, win/lose model of power is a way of life that existed long before video games. This classic model for power struggles, punctuated by skirmishes for control, can edge immature people with poor impulse control into violence.

We cannot have healthy relationships if people are always on guard or attacking/counter-attacking. We cannot have a win-win family if we constantly make others wrong so that we can be right. We cannot have healthy children if they get unhealthy messages and operate from a distorted value system which they consider to be "normal".

There are basically two power games we can play:

- **Power Sharing.** Based on respect, caring, compassion and support, people share power with each other. Cooperative, mutual, nurturing partnerships enhance and expand everyone's personal power. As people share power, the power increases.
- **Power Taking.** People lacking a sense of personal power often try to get it at another's expense. They dominate and disempower others. They may use any means, including violence, to gain control. In their

'me vs. you' thinking, they put others down to feel one up. Always competing with others, they think they are okay *if* they are better than, stronger than, smarter than others. They try to feel good at someone else's expense; but it doesn't work. Self-esteem in not possible in this very common, win-lose power struggle. One person may appear to win, but the other is resentful. No one actually wins.

When we view power competitively, in up-down/win-lose terms, the idea of kids, wives, or husbands having power may be seen as a personal threat. Aware of only two options, parents (or siblings) not wanting to lose will fight to keep others from winning.

When we move beyond the dominating/submissive definition of power, however, we discover that giving Johnny and Suzie a sense of their own power does not take it away from Mom and Dad. We build a family in which people are *for,* not against each other. Just as all citizens have rights in a democratic society, a winning family honors the rights of every member.

In the divorce arena power games can result in parents fighting to win a custody battle with little regard for what is best for their children. Children are the victims in this win-lose system. A positive alternative to a legal battle is mediation in which a skilled mediator helps both parties figure out what is best for them *and* for the children.

Four Dimensions of Power

Imagine four people in a room together, each representing one stop on the spectrum of power. There's M. Powerless, who is helpless, dependant, insecure, and uninformed. There's M. Powerful, who is confident, capable, in control, and a risk-taker. M. Empowering is supportive, encouraging, and challenging. M. Overpowering is dominating, manipulative, arrogant, and pushy. Who would be attracted to each other? If each one brought their spouse, what would they be like? Who would be drawn together? Who would avoid each other?

We have all been affected or hurt in some way by an overpowering person—a parent, teacher, friend, boss, or even a stranger. The object of their game is to gain power at another's expense. Some common tactics include: belittling, demoralizing and discouraging, changing the rules, withholding support, intimidation, keeping secrets, and blocking/weakening/destroying connections.

"Divide and conquer" is an ancient strategy that is used around the world and still happens today in our own society. We have been fragmented from family and friends, from our ethnic roots, from our communities and neighborhoods, from Mother Earth. In the name of individuality, competion, and progress, we have been separated from other ethnic groups believing that their well-being directly threatens our own. Constantly on the move, many people feel alienated, disconnected, and lonely.

Reconnecting and Mending

If we have lost our power by being divided and conquered, we can regain it by reclaiming and mending our missing pieces. We can gain power by turning to others like ourselves to share our common experience. As we connect with others, we can heal ourselves and increase our power.

In a Mexican barrio, a pastoral worker gathered together women living in the same area. Although they lived very close to one another, they didn't know each other at all. As they sewed together, they discovered they had things in common. Each one was being battered. They realized that they were not alone, or crazy, or at fault.

They decided to do something to stop the abuse. Each woman got a whistle. They pledged that if any of them was abused, they or one of their kids would blow the whistle. The other women would immediately gather around her house in a circle banging on pots and pans. "That simple and empowering action began to transform the cycle of abuse in the barrio and change the relationships fostered among the women, within other relationships, and in how they saw themselves and their own power."[2] The single action of telling the truth led them out of isolation and into empowerment.

If we have been divided from ourselves—from our bodies, minds, emotions, spirituality—we can regain our power by reclaiming the missing pieces. When we accept our negative and abused parts and forgive ourselves, we become integrated and whole. As we love and embrace our wounded inner child, we can heal our lives. In honoring, supporting, and having compassion for ourselves and others, we can tap into our deepest power. From this source of strength we can draw the courage to meet life's challenges.

Violence: The Abuse of Power

Of all the industrialized nations, the United States is the most violent.[3] Women and children are the primary victims. Men are the primary perpetrators. Conditioned to accept violence and trained to commit violence, men have difficulty talking about how it has affected them—as targets of violence, as victims of child abuse, rape, and war.

Violence is the number one health hazard in this country, more threatening than cancer, heart disease, or even automobiles. And it is addictive. Although violence in the home is a difficult issue to address, it must be discussed. Silence means acquiescence, tolerance, and acceptance.

- Next to illness, the number one cause of death in children under one year of age is homicide.[4]
- One out of three girls and one out of six boys face sexual abuse in some form before the age of eighteen.
- The greatest single cause of injury in women is battering.

Children raised in violent homes are victims. They learn violence as a way of life. They do unto others what was done unto them or what their parents did to each other, and the violence repeats. Studies show that boys raised in violent households become perpetrators, while their sisters learn to accept abuse by others.

Violence of all kinds is reaching epidemic proportions in American families. When children are abused, as adults their inner rage threatens us all. Abusive families therefore are public, not private problems; they affect all levels of society.

Violence has become so widespread in our society that we have come to accept it as "normal". More violent deaths occur annually in New York City than have occurred in the last thirty years of war in Ireland! This is not "normal." The leading cause of death of young black men is homicide. This is not "normal."

The former Chief of Police of Minneapolis, Anthony V. Bouza, commented on these concerns at a National Conference on Violence: "For centuries women have been raised to accept their fate as victims and therefore to think and act like victims. If they were abused, they were led to believe that they somehow 'deserved' it. But those days have got to end for all women."

According to Bouza, the police, the criminal justice system and others "must abandon their convenient myths of male authority and power"[5] and must treat women differently. This does not just mean respect; it means sharing power. When women are put on a pedestal, they are set up to disappoint others and thus "deserve" punishment. In countries where women are valued and empowered, crime against women is not a problem. In winning families both husband and wife have dignity and equal importance. The work and contributions of each are valued and appreciated.

If you live in an abusive home, be responsible for your own safety and that of your children. It is essential that you find someone to talk to. Get help. Visualize what you want for yourself, and find the courage to make the choices you need to. Think about timing. Protect yourself and your kids from harm. This is your right.

If you were raised in an abusive family, instead of repeating the mistakes, you can learn from them. Remember what it was like for you. Instead of wounding your children, you can heal yourself. You didn't deserve the abuse you received; neither do your kids. Seek information and treatment. Get supports. Believe in yourself. Develop a vision of hope to move away from the destructive patterns of your past.

Gender Definitions

The ideal, romantic view of the sexes in our culture defines masculine as dominating, superior, and controlling; in other words, to be masculine means to be overpowering. When boys act in these ways, parents may say "Boys will be boys" and let them escape consequences. The romantic definition of feminine is passive, pleasing, sweet, obliging; in other words, to be feminine means to be powerless; and parents smile in approval at the nice little girls. These romantic cultural definitions of power lock us into unhealthy interpersonal win/lose power struggles. They teach us to create dysfunctional families.

Yet at different times and in different cultures, children have grown up in less restrictive cultural molds. I was amazed to learn that the word virile comes from the same Latin root as the word virtue! To be an adult male had other healthier expectations then. And in ancient cultures, the word power meant "to serve." Author Paula Gunn Allen discussed images of male power in her Native American tradition.[6]

> "A man, if he's a mature adult, nurtures life. He does rituals that will help things grow, he helps raise the kids, and he protects the people. His entire life is toward balance and cooperativeness. The ideal of manhood is the same as the ideal of womanhood. You are autonomous, self-directing, and responsible for the spiritual, social and material life of all those with whom you live."

More and more men are rethinking and challenging the restrictive cultural definitions of manhood. Realizing that the economic security of the family is not the only or most important domain, they are rediscovering their innate capacity to bond with and nurture their children. They are tapping freeze-dried parts of themselves and are making new choices. Men are learning to be friends and important resources for each other. And more and more couples are striving for partnership relationships where they share power rather than fight for it.

Family Empowerment

On the national level, parents are collaborating to help each other constructively address their needs. Parent Action, a division of the Family Resource Coalition, is a newly formed national lobby dealing with the concerns and well-being of the 35 million families in the United States with children under eighteen. Connecting with others, parents can now begin to shape a unified voice and a vision of empowerment.[7]

Dr. T. Berry Brazelton, Parent Action co-chair, pediatrician and author, states, "I want to empower young parents to get in there and get what they need. I want to fight for parent power. Our culture is in grave danger and it's because we're not paying enough attention to strengthening our families."[8]

The family unit is a basic building block in society. Traditionally, it has been a source of identity, strength, and stability for its individual members and the community at large. If a family is a battle ground for personal power struggles, people are victimized. When, on the other hand, members of a family feel a sense of personal power, they don't have to fight for it. Husbands and wives can empower each other in an egalitarian relationship. They can empower their children and see to it that everyone can get their needs met and no one is victimized. Powerful families, in which members share power, can renew the entire society.

As parents we have tremendous power over our children's lives. We can empower children by offering them choices, and by encouraging them to be strong and smart. We can also empower them by teaching them

- to be respectful—of themselves and others
- to be responsible for their behaviors
- that they have personal body rights
- to be assertive
- to be sensitive
- to be non-violent
- to avoid dangers but to fight their battles

We can raise our sons to be sensitive and strong men who are not abusive. We can raise our daughters to be strong women who will not be battered. We teach these things best when we honor these qualities in our families and model them in our own relationships.

High self-esteem people who value themselves and others do not tolerate abuse. They know they don't deserve it.

Our homes can be a refuge—a haven of love and safety, a source of strength and support. You have the power to create a supportive and peaceful family where people are for, not against, each other. Children need to feel safe at home. So do you.

13.

For Your Own Good: Discipline Without Damage

"Why do I so frequently need to be protected from those who love me?"

—Ashleigh Brilliant [1]

"Spare the rod and spoil the child." We all heard it when we were young. Most people understood it to mean that if you don't want a spoiled child—obnoxious, surly, and nasty—you've got to spank them once in awhile. The original meaning of this saying is quite the opposite, however. Biblical scholars tell us that shepherds in earlier times had two tools—a staff and a rod. Contrary to modern belief, the rod was not used for hitting; it was used gently—to guide the sheep in the desired direction.

Looking at the statement with new eyes, it rings even more true. Children need to be guided. If they are not guided—or if they are misguided—they will be "spoiled". Children cannot be spoiled by loving them too much. They are spoiled by a *lack* of love and guidance.

It is tragic that the original meaning of this quotation has been twisted to justify child abuse. By trying to not spoil children, parents have damaged them, instead.

The word *discipline* is also frequently misinterpreted. When I ask parents what comes to mind when they hear that word, they respond with "punishment," "force," and "hitting."

79

Yet the word *discipline* has the same root as the word *disciple,* meaning *pupil* or *learner.* The purpose of discipline is to teach in such a way that children can learn, and to help children develop their *inner* guidance system so they can function responsibly by themselves. They need to learn self-discipline with little things so they have the strength to deal with larger issues later on.

The short-term goal of discipline is to guide behavior on a daily basis and to protect children from hurting themselves and others. In the long run, discipline should help children become self-disciplined and take over the responsibility for their own behavior. They need to learn to rely on themselves, but this process takes time.

Natural and Logical Consequences

In rural settings, natural consequences are a natural occurrence. If you conscientiously tend your garden, there will be a bountiful harvest. If you neglect to milk the cow, she will dry up. The connections are direct and clear.

In some settings, individuals in families, neighborhoods, and communities function as parts of interdependent systems and are accountable to each other. Extended families provide diverse role models, and there is a sense of connection even between unrelated adults and children. For individuals today, however, this lifestyle is the exception rather than the rule.

Today, children have fewer adults involved in their lives. Interaction time with parents is often minimal. They spend more and more of their time in front of the TV. Most television programs, however, do not teach natural consequences—the pain, burials, re-buildings that would happen *after* the story ends. Children miss learning about the cause-effect, action-reaction cycles of life. Removed from the lessons of *natural* consequences, we must rely on *logical* consequences in teaching these skills.

Logical consequences[2] are structured situations based on mutual rights and mutual respect, that permit children to learn from the reality of the social order. One day, for example, while doing errands with my young children, they started fighting in the back seat of the car. I was distracted and irritated and could easily have yelled at them, "You're going to lose your allowance," "You're grounded," or some other threat of punishment. Instead, I pulled the car off the road and turned off the engine. Very soon they stopped and asked, "What happened, Mom?" I softly explained that I couldn't drive with so much noise because it distracted me; I would have to wait until they quieted down. It worked like a charm—for about two miles. After a few repeats, they got the point.

It's important to have fair rules and to state them clearly so everyone understands. It's also important that children see the connection between cause and effect—rowdiness, for example, causes Mom to pull the car off the road.

When they know what is expected and don't comply with the rules, they learn from the consequences of their behavior. Consequences must be related, respectful, and reasonable. When children know what is expected and comply with the rules, there can be a sense of accomplishment, importance, and increased self-esteem.

Rescue Behavior

It is easy to interrupt the natural process of learning from consequences. When we rescue others, they miss out on important lessons. The undesirable behavior is therefore likely to be repeated.

Rescue Behavior

	Case 1	Case 2
Action	Child turns off alarm.	Child spends money without anticipating future needs.
Result	Oversleeps, misses school bus.	Wants money for activity; has no money left.
Logical Consequence	Child must walk, bike, or take city bus; is late for school.	Child misses activity or has to earn extra money.
Rescuing Action	Parent drives child to school.	Parent gives child money.

The choice not to rescue takes a strong commitment to helping children learn about life from their own behaviors and from the social system. It must be appropriate both to the age and maturity level of the child and to the situation. It must also be done in an atmosphere of dignity and respect, love and firmness. The "art of parenting"—including wisdom and good judgment—are part of the picture.

There are times when every parent chooses to practice rescue behavior. Sometimes situations occur that are damaging or difficult for a child to handle. A child being bullied or abused may not have the internal resources to deal with it. There are times when we need to rescue our children.

There may be times when grownups need to be rescued, too. Sometimes life deals us a hard blow; it's wonderful to know there are people we can call on when we're down and out. People get stronger by asking for help and support once in a while—until they get the strength to move on. The problem occurs when rescuing becomes a way of life, when someone always looks to others to take charge and solve problems. This behavior pattern disempowers, weakens, and creates low self-esteem and dependency.

Rewards and Punishment

"The fundamental issue is not punishment at all, but the development of morality—that is, the creation of conditions that not only allow but strongly induce a child to wish to be a moral, [self-] disciplined person."

— Bruno Bettelheim[3]

Most of us at one time or another have experienced the reward and punishment system, i.e., a star or a slap for our behavior. It is based on external control, relying heavily on fear, anger, disappointment, and guilt. Yet parents who rely on punshment may believe their children *are* bad, and try to make them good by making them feel bad. But when we feel bad, it's easier to do bad things. Some of the major disadvantages of the reward and punishment system are:

- Parents are assumed to be responsible for their children's behavior. They consider the children's performance or misbehavior to be a reflection on them. The parent feels guilty for a child's mistakes and asks, "Where did I go wrong?"
- Parents make all the rules and decisions and expect compliance, which almost inevitably leads to resistance.
- Children are prevented from making their own judgments and decisions and therefore from defining their own standards of behavior.
- Parents use negative strategies to enforce their will: yelling, ridicule, criticism, blame, put-downs, labeling—all of which damage self-esteem.
- If a behavior is controlled by an authority figure, it usually lasts only while the authority figure is present.

When looking at rewards and punishment, it is important once again to remember that children observe first, then conclude. More often than not, the "lessons" children learn from punishment are not at all what the parents had hoped to teach. A thirty-four-year-old woman told me that she vividly remembers the time her parents sent her down to the bottom basement stair to finish her dinner after she complained that she couldn't chew the meat left on her plate because it was too gristly. When I asked her what she learned from that, she said, "I learned that my parents didn't believe me, even if I was telling the truth. I learned that I was less important than their 'clean your plate' rules, and I hated them for humiliating me."

The intention of the parent, to stop unacceptable behavior, is honorable, but the way they go about it leaves something to be desired. The goal of punishment is to force submission ("I'll show you who's boss") or to get retaliation. They may stop the behavior and damage the child and the relationship in the process. When children are deliberately hurt by parents whom they trust, love, and depend upon, they receive a powerful negative message. Observing and feeling their mistreatment, they may conclude that

- they are not okay; they are bad.
- they don't deserve love; they deserve hate.
- their parents hate them.
- their parents are bad, cruel.
- they deserve to be punished.
- they cannot trust the parent.
- it's okay to hurt people.
- the world is not a safe place.

When these conclusions become their truth, when they believe that they deserve it, they may create punishing relationships (for themselves or others) throughout their lives.

Think back to a time when you were punished as a child. What were your feelings toward your parent(s)? What did you learn? How did you feel about yourself?

When parents vow "to teach them a lesson," the children probably learn fear, distrust, hatred. When parents use force and violence, they teach children to be violent, or to be victims.

Rewards may not seem on the surface to be as potentially damaging as punishment, but they often produce similar results. Children begin to feel manipulated; they learn that they have to "perform" to win their parents' attention and approval. They learn to become people pleasers. After a time, they come to resent the rewards as much as the punishments.

Creative Family Management

Many parents are in the habit of using the reward and punishment system. They often repeat what *their* parents did, even though they hated it. Yet, there are many better ways to work with people. Here are some healthier options:

- Suggest. "It might be a good idea_____."
- Ask for a favor or a change in behavior.
- Offer an alternative activity or location. "It's not okay to be so wild in the living room; go play in the yard."
- Say no. "No, you may not do that."
- Communicate clearly what you want and how important it is to you. Eye contact and a touch helps the message get through.
- Remove the temptation. Separate the kid from the problem.
- Substitute. If a child is heading for trouble, head him or her off with something more interesting. If a toddler has found something dangerous, take it away while giving him or her something more fun.
- Team up with them. "Let's pick up the toys together."
- Appreciate and cheer their efforts and their successes. (See Appendix B.)
- Focus on what your children like to do that can happen after something they don't want to do. "If you get your pajamas on fast, we'll have more time to read a good story."
- Use non-verbal signals. I got tired of reminding my young ones to buckle up their safety belts, so I tried something different. I'd tap their legs. They quickly got the message.
- Distract them. Divert their energy. On car rides when the kids were thirsty, I would tell them to lick their lips. It worked many times!
- Outsmart them. When walking with my little nephew, he complained of being tired. I suggested we run instead. It was fun and we got there faster.
- Write notes. I'd jot down chores for my kids to do after school. After establishing this as a form of communication, it became routine.
- Signal. Advance notice is fair and makes good sense in driving and in parenting. Announcing that you have to leave in ten minutes allows kids to shift gears and complete what they're doing. Setting a timer can help to make kids aware of limits.
- Relax your standards. Instead of expecting a perfectly made bed, for example, realize that some ideals are not worth daily battles. Pulling up the blankets was a compromise that worked for me.
- Get a timer. Let kids know how much time they have for an activity, then set the timer.
- "Chunk down" a large task into manageable pieces; encourage them. Celebrate their progress.

- Play (for example turning a toddler's spoon into an airplane full of food, or overdramatizing great disgust and nausea on finding dirty underwear in the bathroom). When I'd notice untied shoelaces on a walk with my children, I'd playfully try to step on them.

There are many ways to get what we want. The methods above avoid direct confrontation and punishment. You can get things done more easily if you avoid power struggles. And self-esteem will remain intact.

With rewards, as with punishment, children learn to focus on trying to please those who have power over them, whether they want to or not: "I will do _____ so you will think I'm okay." When parents give stars for getting dressed, for example, and scoldings for being slow, kids feel manipulated.

A better approach is to peek in on their progress, saying "Hooray, you got your shoes on. Good for you, you're almost ready." Celebrate their progress, their growth. This reflects their small achievements back to them and helps them to intrinsically feel good about themselves. Tomorrow they may tell themselves (self-talk) the same thing: "Good for me, I'm almost ready."

With the reward system, tomorrow the child may again want a star or some other bribe to externally motivate him or her to get dressed. This outside focus leads to the development of external locus of control people (see Chapter 19), who lack self-confidence and always look to others to tell them what to do.

Rewards, in moderation, are okay. Don't stop rewarding your kids. The ultimate goal, though, is for the child *to want to* get dressed, practice piano, or keep his room clean for himself, without involving time or energy on the parent's part. This attitude is more likely to result from the encouragement/support method.

Physical punishment doesn't change someone's mind. It may change behavior for a while, but it doesn't change their opinion or thinking about what they're doing. Fear is a poor motivator.

When people are blamed and punished, they feel as if they have been attacked or violated. They may react by

- being defensive
- making excuses
- trying to protect themselves
- wanting to withdraw
- being afraid
- giving in (complying)
- becoming defiant
- becoming a perfectionist ("If I were perfect, I might be okay.")
- lying, cheating, or covering up

85

Once parents decide that they want children to be self-disciplined, they must discipline themselves to change old, punishing patterns of behavior and to model new behaviors. Once parents decide that they do not need to control—that they can trust children to learn from the consequences of their behavior—they can give up punishments and the associated feelings of distrust and resentment. They can move from an autocratic to a more democratic leadership style. With the natural/logical consequences approach,

- children are responsible for their own behavior.
- they are allowed to make their own decisions and to learn from their successes and their mistakes.
- children learn from the reality of the natural and social order rather than from forced compliance to the wishes of authority figures.

This system of discipline focuses on the whole child—not only on behavior. The goal is to teach *self*-discipline, *self*-direction, and *self*-responsibility. Since parents won't always be around to tell children what to do, they must instill *inner* discipline and help the children develop the ability to think, to judge, and to make decisions on their own. They must also model the behavior they want to see in their children: example is the best teacher.

"It is easier to control than to teach," writes Dr. Stephen Glenn, an author and national consultant. "Teaching requires time, planning and patience, but it lasts longer, gives clearer direction, and builds a foundation for a system of value. Dogs need to be controlled. Children need to be taught."[4]

Parents must realize that every child is frisky and mischievous at times. It is how they express their individuality and aliveness. If they want to do something and it doesn't hurt them, let them do it. Give them the freedom to be who they are. All normal kids act out once in a while; they are testing their environment. It's important to allow them self-expression while also setting limits.

When I had two little ones, I made up a name—"Boobledink"—to express mild displeasure. If, for example, someone would poke a finger in the icing of a birthday cake, I'd say, "You Boobledink," with partly serious displeasure. It helped make a point and kept me from using hurtful labels such as "bad." "brat," "idiot". Even now, I sometimes call my grown children that, and we laugh about it.

It's important to be aware of the degree of seriousness of the mischief. If it's serious, it should be dealt with, but there may be wisdom in letting little things slide. *Choose your battles carefully.*

It's also important to look for the cause of undesirable behavior and deal with that. Misbehavior is a signal that something isn't right.

Play detective; figure out what good reason they might have for that behavior. They may be tired, hungry, or reacting to something in their diet. Or they may need attention, be discouraged, or feel powerless. Get to the underlying feelings. *Help them to talk it out so they don't have to act it out.*

The democratic family is a family where no one has to lose. It is a winning team in which parents are coaches who are positive, encouraging, and correcting when necessary. Kids need attention, feedback, and the awareness that they are fulfilling your expectations. Parents who are coaches get positive results.

Coaches expect the best in their players and communicate that to their team. They believe in them and inspire them to greatness. The team members don't want to disappoint the coach, so they do their best.

Coaches are teachers who explain how to do things better. One dad, for example, observed his daughter using a hammer. Seeing her ineffectiveness, he stopped her, took the hammer, and showed her the correct way to use it. Giving it back to her, he asked her to try it that way. As she hammered more effectively, Dad encouraged her and celebrated her success.

Look for opportunities to share your knowledge and your skills. You know so much, and your children have so much to learn. Teaching them empowers them and sets up positive contact between you.

Finally, coaches spend time correcting undesirable and unacceptable behavior. They do that without discouraging or demoralizing the player. *In The One-Minute Manager*, Kenneth Blanchard and Spencer Johnson[5] outline this simple plan:

1. Let them know you want them to learn and grow and that you will correct them at times. Correcting them does not mean you don't like them or that you're rejecting them but that there's a better way.
2. Correct behavior while it's happening or as soon as you are aware of it. Deal with them in private.
3. Tell them that what they did was not acceptable. Describe the behavior, being specific, firm, and kind.
4. Tell them what you think and feel about that behavior, being clear but not angry.
5. Pause and let it soak in.
6. Touch them, smile, or say kind words to show you have not rejected them, that you are on their side. Tell them that you value them but that the specific behavior is unacceptable.
7. Forgive and forget it. It's over.

We must deal with unacceptable behavior—in our kids, spouses, and friends, and in ourselves. How we do this makes a difference. If we do so in a caring, firm way—and keeping our sense of humor—we can make a difference in the self-esteem of our children.

If I keep from commanding people, they behave themselves.

If I keep from preaching at people, they improve themselves.

If I keep from imposing on people, they become themselves.

—Lao Tsu

14.

Guidance

"If this is the age of television, I intend to find another age to live in."
—Garrison Keeler[1]

On a trip to Nepal, I visited a village at the edge of a jungle inhabited by rhinos, tigers, and wild boars. In the river there were crocodiles. Children growing up in that environment are surrounded by imminent dangers—and learn very early how to avoid them. Everyone in the village knows that the rhinos leave their feeding ground after dark to go elsewhere to sleep. Young children must be taught—as I was taught—to stay off the path when the rhinos might be there. They must learn how to avoid dangerous animals and, if necessary, how to deal with them. Nepalese children taught me what to do if I were to meet a rhino—climb a tree fast!

Every culture has teachings that are transmitted from parent to child. American parents don't have to teach their kids how to deal with rhinos, but they need to guide them in many other ways. Parents need to forewarn their children and protect them from the numerous hazards built in to the urban, suburban, and rural environment. There are poisons under the kitchen sink and in the medicine cabinet, pollutants seeping into the water, and escaping into the air. Never before has a generation of children been forced to wonder whether the Earth would die beneath its feet.

The social world is also very frightening. Parents are concerned about the dangers that seem to lurk just beyond the playground. Kids are scared, too.

In the past, a skull and crossbones marked household dangers, such as iodine, in the medicine cabinet. Now, kids use that symbol as a decoration for their skateboards and clothing. We need to again name the danger—the poisons—for ourselves and our children. Instead of indulging in worry, we can turn our concern into positive action.

Children look to parents for guidance. They want it, and they need it. In the past, parents were the primary teachers of values, appropriate behavior and lifeskills. Children used to spend most of their waking hours interacting with parents, grandparents, and other members of their extended family. Now they spend most of their waking hours watching television.

A study done in Boston revealed that by the time a child reaches age eighteen, he or she has viewed 350,000 commercials. The average American watches television six hours and twenty minutes per day. During those many hours, they sit back and wait for things to happen; they are passive and uninvolved. They take in whatever happens to be showing, whether they like it or not, whether it's true or not, whether it's healthy or not. At the time of life when their minds are most impressionable and receptive, children are being "parented" by television.

As a project for an anthropology class, I joined my children (then eight through twelve years old) for Saturday morning cartoons. Within three hours, we counted forty-two commercials, mostly aimed at influencing children's food choices and parents' buying habits. Together we rated the quality and agreed that only two of the programs were amusing; the rest were mediocre to poor, often using slapstick or violence as humor. By about 11:00 A.M., I was beginning to feel a bit nauseous (and a little "crazy"), so I turned it off. My kids protested, saying, "Mom, maybe the next one will be better."

A report by the University of Pennsylvania's School of Communication recently stated that the "family hour" on TV (which has the most children viewers) is really the "violence hour." The programs of the three major networks include 168 acts of violence per week. This is the highest rate of violence in the nineteen years since the study was first conducted in 1967.[2] More people can see the worst TV program in one evening than could see a Broadway show playing to a full house for twenty years.

Advertisers, in their competition for the consumer dollar, are becoming more and more skillful at manipulating the viewing public. They have confused us and undermined our self-esteem, blurring the distinction between real and artificially manufactured "needs." Traveling to other countries points up the absurdity of our consumer mentality. We do not *need* designer clothes and VCRs; kids do not *need* a Nintendo System. Our real needs are rather simple: food and shelter, safety, belonging, love, respect, self-esteem. All other "needs" are really only wants/desires/ wishes—or things we're being talked into thinking we have to have.

The hours spent viewing TV are hours not available for actively participating in the real world, or playing, or being involved with friends and family. Watching television is an individual activity that tends to discourage interaction with others; as viewing time increases, family communication time decreases. As family communication decreases, people grow more distant from each other and may even forget how to carry on a good conversation.

Young children need to learn about life, about how this world works, about how to think, feel, and behave. Impressionable and trusting, they watch television to learn appropriate behavior, skills, and values. Information and misinformation alike become part of their reality, their belief system. They are innocent; they are vulnerable.

The unconscious cannot distinguish between fact and nonfact, between fantasy and reality. It accepts everything as truth, even that which is not true. (See Chapter 17.) In good faith, children take in and believe what they are "taught." They may be more likely to internalize TV values than to believe their own experience—or what their parents teach them. This TV version of reality can and does lead to confusion, pain, and addiction. For children raised on a heavy TV diet, television replaces direct firsthand experiencing and becomes their reality.

When children look to television to learn about life, what do they learn? They learn to become consumers—never to be satisfied with what they have, always to "need" more things; then they become frustrated and angry if they cannot afford them. They learn to crave sugar. They learn to seek immediate gratification of their desires and quick solutions to their problems—violence, perhaps—or they learn to be passive and uninvolved with life. They also learn that

- Happiness comes from material possessions and external conditions.
- Drugs will cure everything.
- Violence is exciting and acceptable behavior.
- Our homes are infested with dirt and invisible enemies that the housewife must continually work to eliminate.
- Skinny is beautiful, and women's bodies are never okay as they are.

These ideas are all setups for low self-esteem. They are accepted in good faith by children hungry to understand life and how they should be in their world. Their minds are filled with misinformation that they consider to be true.

A task force of the American Academy of Pediatrics concluded after a sixteen-month study that

- "Repeated exposure to TV violence can make children both violent and accepting of real-life violence.
- "TV-watching promotes obesity.
- "TV encourages the use of drugs, alcohol and tobacco by glamorizing them.
- "TV's unrealistic sexual relationships may contribute to the risk of teen pregnancy."[3]

Most network TV producers and programmers have no commitment to the guidance of children. Their commitment is to their advertisers–to get viewers to buy products. They show programs to draw consumer audiences, and accept no responsibility for the immense impact of those programs or advertisements on our children. At this time, however, there are some changes occurring in advertisements. For example, the many years of work on the part of Mothers Against Drunk Drivers (MADD) and other groups are beginning to pay off as alcohol advertisers must now comply with stricter guidelines, and are starting to encourage more responsible drinking.

I remember life before television. As kids we had lots of time to play—times that were perhaps the happiest of my childhood. We would roller-skate, ride bikes, and go on snakehunts. We learned to entertain ourselves. With television, this has all changed.

People who grow up without television gain firsthand, hands-on experience of the world. They spend more time actively interacting with people and participating in life. They have a more solid foundation.

We learn from everything. So do children. Do you trust TV to teach your children? Do you know what they are watching? Get involved—choose programs to watch together. There are many fine programs on science, art, culture, entertainment, music, and sports. Help your kids select the best, and limit viewing time. Properly regulated, TV can enhance your family's life—as can many other activities.

I heard a story about someone who visited a home while children were watching a mystery on TV. Suddenly there were cries of "Don't do it!" "Don't hurt him!" Questioning the mother, the visitor found out that she usually turned off programs at the onset of violence.

Children need the benefit of our experience, our wisdom, and our protection so they won't be damaged. As parents we need to protect the innocence of young children. They need our proactive leadership to help them avoid or deal with the hazards of daily living. When we actively guide them, we steer them away from many potential problems and the resulting stress and trauma.

Children also need guidance to understand themselves and the world they live in, to help them handle their physical, social, and sexual development. It takes courage for parents to talk about some of these things. But if kids can't talk with their own parents, who *will* they talk to? What will they learn? Who will they learn from?

With thoughtful guidance, we can save our children from preventable pain and nudge them to become healthy, responsible people with high self-esteem.

"If not you, who? If not now, when?"

—Hillel

15.

Problem Solving

*"To the questions of your life, you are the only answer.
To the problems of your life, you are the only solution."*

—Jo Coudert[1]

When I was a child and my brothers teased me, I ran to my mother wanting protection for me and punishment for them. When I had misunderstandings with my friends, I would not play with them again—or at least not until we forgot about it. I ran away from and avoided problems because I never learned how to face them and get through them. I was unprepared for the challenges of the world and was afraid of them.

As a mother, however, I didn't want my kids to pull me into the middle of every argument they had. I wanted them to be able to solve their own disagreements by themselves. A friend with many adopted children once told me her secret formula: whenever two children had a problem, she had them sit on a certain stair—"the stair of love and peace"—until they worked it through; then they could go play. Those children learned to resolve problems by themselves.

I tried this on my own children. Although they hated that stair, they soon learned that *they* were responsible for solving their problems. In effect, I stepped aside and allowed them to develop important skills. In learning to solve their little problems, they began to gain the skills, experience, and confidence to solve the tougher problems of life.

Problems and conflicts are natural events in life. Everyone has them. We don't choose hassles, but we do choose how to deal with them. Some strategies intensify the problem and cause distance, distress, and low self-esteem. Other strategies reduce the intensity and bring about resolution, closeness, and joy. Without skills and confidence, every problem is a crisis. With skills and confidence, a problem is a challenge to take on, an event to deal with and get beyond.

It's easy to feel responsible for solving other people's problems. Yet this isn't necessarily a good thing. If we solve problems *for* them, we deprive them of the opportunity to gain competence, confidence, and personal power. In addition, our solutions may not be the best solution for them.

Ask: Whose problem is this? *That* person is responsible for the solution. We can listen as they talk through their troubles. This often begins to alleviate the problem. It lets them know we care, lets them hear themselves and helps them get perspective. Then, ask what *they* can do to resolve *their* issue.

Children need to learn to take care of their own problems—and to overcome them. They need to learn to deal with disappointments, losses, and pain so that they know they can survive them. It can be difficult for us as parents to watch them struggle; we want to take away the pain. Yet children who have been overprotected will be incapacitated and overwhelmed by the first real problem they have to handle on their own. Kids who don't know how to deal with failure, disappointment, or loss are at risk.

We need to encourage and support children through their struggles—and believe in them. ("I've seen you solve some tough problems; I know you can get through this one, too.") We need to allow them to experience their own mistakes and failures and help them discover the joy of overcoming. It is not problems that overwhelm kids but self-doubt, and lack of experience and skills.

We need to share our own struggles with our children. If we pretend to have it together all the time, they may conclude that something's wrong with them for having problems. When we share our mistakes, our losses, our failures, and how we deal with them, they understand that we, too, experience disappointments—that we, too, are human. And they learn new ways of coping.

Adults and children alike have basic human needs, including safety, love, attention, belonging, and esteem. If we ignore these needs, problems often result. Misbehavior may be a signal that children's needs are not being met. When we attend to these needs, we avoid potential problems.

In dealing with family problems, it is important to listen to each other, to understand the situation clearly, and to have the willingness and courage to make changes. When all parties assume responsibility for the problem *and* the resolution, there's hope for a positive outcome.

One adolescent exhibited problem behavior as a result of the stresses of her family situation. She wrote

> My 'family' became a constant clash of rage caused and aggravated by lying, mistrust, and hurtful accusations. I was driven out by hatred based on something I don't understand. In my self-destructive family it became clear that steps had to be taken to alleviate or avoid

further stress. We created commotions, such as fussing, threatening, and running away (behaviors we had never before considered), desperate for a listening ear. We pleaded for either a solution or an escape, and ended up escaping from the problems which were beyond our control.

Her acting out was merely a symptom of the real problems which her parents refused to discuss or deal with. Running away from home was the best solution to a family problem beyond her control.

It is important to understand that there are always reasons—thoughts and feelings—underneath problems and misbehavior. Problems and misbehavior are but signals that indicate that something is wrong. In order to resolve them effectively, we must play detective and figure out what's really going on from the child's point of view.

Barriers to Problem Solving

One reason that people are afraid of problems is that they don't know how to solve them. They may be using one of these strategies

- **Denial.** Although putting problems aside for a little while may help us to cope, we can't get *through* our problems if our head is in the sand. And if it gets stuck there, we're in real trouble!
- **Drugging.** This strategy alters the inner reality—the *perception*

of the problem. With alcohol and other drugs, people can pretend that they've solved the problem because they can no longer feel it. Unfortunately, they are creating a more serious problem of addiction.

- **Distraction.** This strategy of avoidance can be a short- or long-term escape from the problem. ("Let's watch TV.")
- **Gunny-sacking.** Storing up the problems, anger, and pain solves nothing. When it builds up, a harmful explosion may result.
- **Blaming.** When we point our finger at others and resort to fault-finding, we deny our own responsibility and our ability to change things. The persons who are blamed feel attacked and want to either counterattack or defend themselves.
- **Rejection.** Cutting people off may *seem* to solve a problem, but an important relationship can be damaged or lost. ("I never want to see you again.") Sometimes you may need time away from people you love; that's okay. But rejecting a person or a relationship can make life painful.
- **Fighting/Withdrawing.** One is aggressive; the other is passive. In our culture boys are often taught to slug it out, while girls learn to seek help or wait to be rescued. ("Put up your dukes!" or "Mommy! Help me!") Each of these behaviors, used alone, can become a trap.
- **Personal attacks.** Name-calling and you-statements hurt the other, escalate the conflict, and often harm the relationship. ("You are totally worthless.") Often we regret it later.
- **Rationalizing.** This strategy intellectualizes the pain to avoid feeling it. ("We're better off than the Joneses.") This only perpetuates the problem.
- **Defeatism.** If you believe there is nothing you can do to solve the problem, you will not be able to do anything. ("It's hopeless.") You will stay helpless.

These are strategies for living with—not dealing with—problems. They are very common and they get us stuck. We may go through any of these states at one time or another, but they don't work ultimately because they avoid the problem. Avoidance is a cop-out. To cope with and resolve problems, we must *attend* to them.

Many of these strategies go along with the win-lose approach. The goal is to "win" by proving that I am right and you are wrong. Yet no one likes to lose; no one likes to be made wrong. An emotionally charged power struggle ensues from a win-lose solution and often escalates. Everyone's self-esteem is at stake: "If I don't win, I'm not okay; therefore I must win." The problem may appear to be settled, but it isn't because the loser is angry and resentful. No one comes out winning.

A divorce, for example, can be a frightening power struggle. The parents may fight to win a custody battle even though they don't want the primary responsibility for raising their children. The kids get victimized in this wrenching process. Nobody wins. Everybody suffers.

When facing a problem, it helps to examine the underlying goal. Do you want to "win" at the other's expense? Or do you want to resolve it to everyone's satisfaction?

It *is* possible to solve problems with no one losing. Win-win solutions take time, energy, and self-discipline. Sometimes we have to bite our tongues so they don't get us into trouble. Win-win problem solving calls for direct, honest, and assertive communication, and willingness to really listen and *understand* each other. It takes time, energy, and self-discipline. This approach is not easy, but it's worth it. Increased respect, intimacy, and enhanced self-esteem are the payoff.

The goal of win-win strategies is to resolve the problem so that both parties are satisfied. The focus is not on the persons, but on the solution—"What will we *do* about it?" The underlying attitude is respect—for oneself and for the other. Both must accept responsibility for the problem and be committed to resolving it without damaging the relationship.

Stepping Stones to Problem Solving

- Believe that your problem is solvable. Be positive, hopeful, and expect good things to come of it.
- Determine ownership—whose problem is it? Everyone is responsible for solving his or her own problems. Don't solve kids' problems for them—unless they are in danger or in a situation that is bigger than they can handle.
- Don't try to figure out who's right and who's wrong.
- Evaluate the importance of the problem. Tell how important it is. "This isn't very important, but I'd like to talk about it," or "This is very important to me!"
- Speak in terms of "I want," "I feel" rather than "You did this" or "You didn't do that." The I-statement model often resolves problem situations.
- Express your beliefs, values, and opinions as your point of view, not as the Truth.
- Listen to feelings.
- Read between the lines. Try to figure out what's going on underneath the words—fear? anger? a power struggle? protection?—and address that.

- Use active listening skills. Try to understand their point of view, their way of seeing it.
- Be sensitive to timing. Use good judgment as to when to talk; if you are unsure, ask, "Is this a good time to talk?" Allow enough time for discussion.
- Respond to the other; don't react.
- Ask for what you want. "I just want you to listen while I tell you what I feel."
- Be willing to make necessary changes.
- Take time out if things get tense. Take a break to cool down. Do something physical to release the tension. Return to problem solving later.
- Check out all assumptions. "Do you mean___?" "Are you saying___?"
- Look for the lesson behind the problem.
- Keep focused in the here and now; pulling up ancient history muddles things.
- Forgive others their mistakes and ask forgiveness for your own.
- Keep a sense of humor—especially laughing at yourself.
- Rule out violence. It does not solve conflicts and always has negative consequences.
- Get help—family mediation or counseling—if you're having trouble resolving problems. Do it soon, before they go too far.

Problem-Solving Model

"You may not be responsible for being down,
but you are responsible for getting up."

—Jesse Jackson[2]

1. Identify and define the problem or conflict. What is really the problem? What exactly is wrong? Identify the problem without blaming. Be aware of everyone's feelings and needs.
2. Brainstorm for possible solutions. Express and record all ideas as fast as you think of them. Sometimes the craziest, wildest ideas become the best with a little fixing up. No judgment or discussion is allowed while brainstorming.
3. Evaluate the alternatives. Look at the consequences of each choice. Would it solve the problem or make it worse? Work together to find a solution acceptable to both parties. Give and take is necessary for a win-win solution.
4. Choose the best solution. Both parties need to find and agree to this solution. Both must be committed to doing it.

5. Implement the solution. What changes need to be made? Who will do what? When will they do it? For how long? In some situations it may help to informally write out an agreement and sign it to avoid confusion. Decide when to evaluate how it's working.
6. Follow-up evaluation. Assess the results. Is the situation better, worse, or the same? If it is better, do you want to extend the contract? If worse, look for another solution from the brainstorming session and implement it. Be persistent until the problem is resolved.

When we know that we can get through conflicts without losing, we have no need to avoid or withdraw from them. When we acquire skills and experience in resolving touchy situations, our confidence grows, as does our self-esteem. And the more we learn, the more we have to teach our children.

16.

Touch

"Emotional CPR: one hug, one deep breath. Repeat." [1]

The recommended daily requirement for hugs is: four per day for survival, eight per day for maintenance, and twelve per day for growth.[2] Touch is vital to life. We need to be caressed, cuddled, and stroked as much as we need food. Babies who are deprived of touch can actually die; lacking stimulation and nurturance, their spines shrivel up.

A scientist from the National Institutes of Health claims that a lack of touch and pleasure during the formative years of life is the principal cause of human violence. He observed that individuals and societies that experience and promote physical pleasure are also peaceful societies. The two exist in one's life in an inverse proportion: "As either violence or pleasure goes up, the other goes down."[3]

Many people suffer from touch disorders: from neglect (insufficient touch), from battering (painful touch of the wrong intensity), and from incest (inappropriate and violating touch). For persons who have been abused, it would make sense that the necessary healing for such damage should come through the same modality. If, for example, the abuse was verbal, then positive, loving words can be very healing. If the abuse was physical, healing can be facilitated through respectful, appropriate, loving touch. Touch can be a cruel and damaging violation of another person, or it can be a nourishing gift of love and pleasure for those we care for. The choice is ours.

We learned about touch from our parents. If they cuddled and hugged us a lot, we learned to enjoy touch. If they didn't touch us at all, we learned either to crave physical contact, or to physically close ourselves off to others. If they punished and abused us—touching us violently—we probably learned to fear and avoid touch. This fear is reinforced by the violent touch seen in the media.

From the media, we learn to equate touch with sex, yet sexual touch is only one of many types of physical expression. The kind of touch we need most is warm, affectionate, casual, and non-sexual. As we understand this, we can unravel the confusion and separate the two in our minds. Touch as an affectionate gesture is an art worth re-learning.

In New Zealand some nurses work with a group of parents who are at risk of abusing their children—because abusive touch was the only touch they had learned. Every week these parents attend a lecture on childrearing, have a cup of tea, and do the following exercise to practice the art of touch in a new, healthy, loving way.[4] Treat your own child or spouse to this New Zealand "Weather Report". It's important to establish that the body receiving this attention is in charge, and should give feedback. ("More!" "Harder." "Softer." "Stop that.") (Remember, the purpose is to inflict pleasure, not pain.)

Snowflakes. Tap fingertips rapidly on the head, shoulders, and back, lightly, like falling snow.
Raindrops. Tap fingertips simultaneously and with greater intensity.
Thunderclaps. With cupped palms, clap hands across the back and shoulders. This makes good noise; be careful not to slap.
Eye of the tornado. Circle your thumbs across the shoulders and down either side of the spine using your fingertips to anchor the motion.
Tidal wave. Slide your hands in long strokes up and down the arms and across the back. Sound effects can be fun here.
Calm after the storm. Rest your hands on the shoulders and breathe deeply. Slowly remove them to about half an inch above the skin for a few moments. Step back slowly—it may feel to them as if your hands are still there![5]

The nurses found this exercise to be a great success. One mother reported that she stifled an urge to hit her baby, and massaged his back instead—with far superior results! One mother in my workshop told us that her child had difficulty getting to sleep. She tried this massage and "he turned into jello and was out." It's an enjoyable, relaxing, and self-esteem enhancing gift—both to give and to get.

In an unusual school program, a professional acupressurist worked on twenty-three special education students with remarkable results: there were significant gains in cognitive, motor, social/emotional and health areas. In other classrooms students have been taught how to push pressure points which block energy and hold tension in the body. When they say "Push my buttons" to a classmate, they get a little massage. Parents and teachers alike have reported immediate improvement in behavior and self-esteem.[6]

Child Abuse

"Those who cannot remember the past are condemned to repeat it."
—George Santayana[7]

Physical, emotional, verbal, and sexual abuse create enormous problems and pain for individuals, families, and all of society. They damage self-esteem and mental health and destroy trust among us. We don't want to hear these things. We don't want to—or are afraid to—talk about them. Yet in order to break the cycle of violence, these things must be discussed.

Sexual child abuse refers to any inappropriate sexual exposure or touch between an adult and a child. It is inappropriate when the child does not understand the nature of the request and/or when the child is coerced through threats or deceit—that is, if an abusive father tells his daughter that this is "normal" affection. It is inappropriate when an adult takes advantage of a child's innocence, needs, or fears. Inappropriate touch by a parent is highly damaging to the child and to the parent-child relationship.[8] There are many reasons that incest has always been taboo in cultures around the world.

Overly severe physical punishment—hitting (with hands, fists, or objects), pinching, burning (with cigarettes, etc.)—is literally torture. It has caused unspeakable harm to individuals and widespread societal violence. Corporal punishment and neglect can lead to psychopathology in children and misery in families. It is not right for people who say they love you to hurt you in the name of discipline.

Authorities estimate that in our country up to 90 percent of murders, rapes and other violent crimes are committed by people who were child-abuse victims themselves. Lee Harvey Oswald, Charles Manson, and Adolf Hitler—to name but three—were all victims of child abuse.

Behavioral patterns are handed down from one generation to the next. Rejected children tend to become rejecting parents; abused children become abusive parents. The patterns tend to repeat—generation after generation—if we don't take the initiative to stop them.

Many of us who were abused as children deny it. Our parents were very important to us; we depended on them for survival. We needed to believe they were good and, therefore, denied the abuse or made up excuses for their behavior—"I deserved what I got." "It was my fault." "I had it coming." It's safer to see ourselves as "bad," than think our parents are "bad."

Many of us don't want to remember the abuse because it was so bad; we may have needed to forget what was done to us. Many of us minimalize the abuse: "It wasn't all that bad." "I was never hospitalized." "It could have been worse." Many of us hold in the old anger afraid that we might explode and hurt someone we love or hurt ourselves.

If we denied the mistreatment, we probably don't recognize that our primary role models were negative. We don't realize, therefore, that we are automatically following those same negative patterns and inflicting the same abuse on our own children. Continuing the habits and repeating old mistakes, however, we become negative models for our own children, and, tragically, the pattern repeats for yet another generation.

As people begin to recognize their patterns, however, they can gain the freedom to choose differently. *With awareness comes choice.* With determination and support from others (perhaps professional therapists), negative situations can be turned around.

> "From early infancy, children of abusing parents are expected to be submissive, respectful, thoughtful and considerate of their parents. It is axiomatic to the child beater that infants and children exist primarily to satisfy parental needs, that children's needs are unimportant and should be disregarded, and that children who do not fulfill these requirements deserve punishment.[9]
>
> Dr. Brandt F. Steele
> (Chief psychiatrist at the National Center
> for the Prevention and Treatment of Child Abuse)

When abuse occurs in families, many of the following traits may be present in the parents. (They may also be present without battering.)

• **A history of battering.** Parents have learned that beating is the "right way" to discipline children. Quick to anger, they may have poor impulse control. Perhaps they learned those behaviors from their own parents, who may also have been abused.

Once we realize that we had negative models, we can begin to change. We can unlearn damaging behaviors and relearn life enhancing ones. Once we have the courage to allow the memories of the past and remember how they harmed us, we can make conscious choices about the future.

• **A distorted view of the child.** Parents may believe that a child is basically bad and deserving of punishment. They may also believe that about themselves. It's easy to be bad when you believe you're a bad person. Parents may justify abusive treatment, claiming it is necessary to prevent evil behavior from developing. A better way to get kids to be good is to believe that they *are* good—and help them believe that about themselves.

• **Unrealistic expectations.** Parents may have expectations of the child—and perhaps of themselves—that are too high or impossible. They don't realize that children are immature. Babies and young children are not always respectful and considerate of their parents. Kids cannot be expected to understand things as adults or to behave like adults. These parents may expect behavior that is developmentally impossible for the child. A six-month-old, for example, cannot be potty trained. They don't realize that children, by definition, are immature, and may inflict severe punishment for minimal infractions.

Parents may also expect a child to fill their needs. A mother, for example, who wants her daughter to love her as her own mother didn't, is asking for the wrong thing. Kids do not exist to satisfy their parents' needs. Parents, however, do exist to satisfy their children's. It's important to remember that you are the grown-up and your children need your love and guidance.

Parents who were not loved as children must also care for their own wounded inner child. In becoming aware of their own unmet needs, they can begin to heal them; they then won't (unconsciously) expect others to parent them.

• **Warmth is lacking.** The parents may not like the child. They may be unaware, unable, or unwilling to relate to and meet their child's emotional needs. Mom may have felt unloved, married for love but found loneliness instead. She—and her child—may give up hope of acceptance and love. Yet, hope is a spark. If you practice acceptance and caring, love will kindle on its own.

• **A negative focus.** The parent seldom notices or mentions any good qualities in the children but rather is always catching them at being bad. He or she may withhold a privilege and love, or isolate the child to teach a lesson. Regardless of the child's efforts to please, the parent may find something to criticize. The child rarely receives praise. Yet kids need appreciation and encouragement, just as parents do. Flip your focus and find one likable or endearing quality about your child—a cute smile, perhaps—and then another, and another. The quality of your interactions will automatically improve.

• **Poor communication skills.** Parents don't know how to really listen to their children. They forget to put themselves in their child's shoes and to see things from their point of view.

Seeing from another's perspective is an important skill—that can be learned. Learning to really listen and to feel empathy and compassion

can begin to transform a negative relationship. (See Chapter 5.).
• **Overuse/abuse of power.** The parents believe children must be taught "who is boss" and should not be allowed to get away with anything. They are righteous about discipline and punishment. The parents may imagine that the child is trying to anger or hurt them, often taking things personally and retaliating violently. ("I'll show you to talk back to me!") Adults lacking self-discipline are dangerous disciplinarians.
• **Overpunishment.** Parents may not be aware of the limits beyond which punishment becomes abuse. For example, ten spankings are too much when one is sufficient. Also, adults may fail to realize that children have a different time sense. For a young child, ten minutes is almost forever! If you sit a child in a corner for an hour, that's abuse. There are better ways to discipline. (See Chapter 12.)
• **Isolation.** The battering family has few close friends, family supports, or social activities. They feel alienated and do not know where to turn for help. One way to begin is with a phone call. Suggest a cup of tea or a walk to the park with someone. Visit a Parents Anonymous meeting in the area. You are not alone!

Each year thousands of children are paralyzed, physically deformed, mentally damaged and killed through abuse. There is a direct cause-effect relationship. When abuse occurs, damage results. Many parents don't realize how fragile a child's body is. Shaking a child can seriously hurt a child, causing mental retardation, permanent brain damage, and death. Striking a child's body is dangerous. One "good" slap on the cheek of a small child can bruise the brain and cause permanent retardation. You must learn to control damaging impulses. If you are afraid of hurting your child, you have reached a turning point. Take time out to cool off. Get away from the dangerous situation. Ask for help. Call the national toll-free number for ChildHelp, a crisis/referral line: 1-800-422-4453. Child abuse is 100% preventable.

People don't generally wake up in the morning saying, "I think I'll whomp my kid today." As the day goes on and stress builds, something or someone "pushes a button" that "triggers" them, and they react. It is important to learn about your buttons and triggers—and how to defuse them. What happened just before you "lost it"? Magnify that moment; unravel it. You can choose to react differently. What can you do to prevent it from happening again? If you need help doing this, get it.

I remember a time many years ago when I got very angry about a mess in the living room. In trying to figure out why I got so angry, I realized that I thought I had to be a "perfect" housewife in order to feel okay. I saw the mess as a sabotage of my struggle for perfection—of my attempt to be okay. Giving this a great deal of thought, I decided that I did not really believe in or want those impossible standards that I'd been trying to live up to, but I did want to feel good about myself—and my kids. I eased my standards of cleanliness to allow everyone to be more comfortable, relaxed, and happy. I also discovered other ways to develop my self-esteem.

That realization helped to stay my hand later when I wanted to punish my children. I learned to stop and think: is a messy house a good enough reason to spank my kids? It had been for my mother, but I chose differently. My house was rarely perfect, but my kids had higher self-esteem.

Our parents raised us the only way they knew how, and we learned to parent from them. Take time to remember not only what they did to you but also its effect on you and on your relationship with them. Remember how it affected your self-esteem. It may be worth it to your child for you to let those memories return.

Our parents made mistakes, but we survived them. All parents make mistakes, but children can be remarkably resilient. Blaming only gets us stuck. It's healthier to forgive our parents and ourselves. *Learn from their mistakes, don't repeat them.* Create the future you deserve and desire for yourself and your family. *Only you can change the course of your personal history. You have the power to do it.* If you need help, get it.

A friend of mine shared her story:

> A battered child myself, I had no awareness of the incredible anger stored inside me until a month or so after my daughter was born. Having been raised with impatience, demands, and punishments, my instinctual behavior was to lash out whenever her needs conflicted with my limits. While in my mind I saw only love for her, I continued to hurt the most precious being in my life.
>
> When she was one and a half, I made a conscious commitment to become the person I knew I could be, which brought me, two years later, to the realization that violation and violence had been passed down the line of women in our family, and that if I did not stop the pattern, the battering tendency would continue with my daughter. I took responsibility for making that change.
>
> It's now been twenty years, and we have created a loving, accepting, respectful, and caring relationship. A long time coming, it has definitely been worth the effort.

Perhaps there is some truth in the biblical saying, "The sins of the father are visitied upon the third and fourth generation." Let this be the last generation. Call it quits for violence in your family. Begin, instead, a cycle of love.

"Love is the answer, whatever the question."

—A Course in Miracles[10]

17.

Beliefs

"Whether you believe you can or believe you can't, you're right."
—Henry Ford[1]

His friends drove the high school senior home from school that autumn day. Soon afterwards, he took his life. A note near his body read, "Life's a bitch, and then you die." Had this classmate of my son's had more positive beliefs, he would still be alive and enjoying his life.

Most of our beliefs are beyond our awareness. They were handed down to us from our parents, teachers, television, and every person we've ever talked to. Unquestioned, our beliefs became our truth. This truth, then, comprises our "life program," which we act out on a day-to-day basis. And as we put our beliefs into action, they become reinforced; they become real.

The beliefs people hold to be true deeply and profoundly affect who they are and what they get out of life. From our earliest decisions, we create a map which we use all our lives—even after it's outdated. Many beliefs are pre-verbal and beyond our awareness. For example, if young children conclude that the world is not safe, they may hold their breath to control their feelings and to numb their fear; in adulthood what may remain of this very early decision is restricted breathing in an aging body that needs all the oxygen it can get. We drag the past with us through our beliefs, expectations, attitudes, and self-talk. All these factors combine to create our reality.

What were your earliest decisions, or "truths", about life? What were your family beliefs? (Remembering the old household rules may help you identify the beliefs.) In a way, it's easier to spend a lifetime living out hand-me-down, outdated beliefs than to uncover and examine your life program. This is important to do, though, because otherwise you stop growing—and the beliefs you pass on to your children may not work in the world they are growing into. Become conscious of your beliefs. Allow them to enter your awareness as bubbles rise to the surface of a pond.

• What do you believe about life? Is it a rat race we must endure?

Or is the universe a friendly place?

- What do you believe about children? Are they senseless little monsters who need to be tamed? Or are they exuberant beings full of life, who need to be guided?
- What do you believe about parenting? Do you believe a mother's duty is to serve her family and a father's is to earn money? Or do parents face a challenge of balancing care-giving and bread-winning in the way most fulfilling to each of them?

If I believe that kids are monsters, I **expect** trouble. Irritation, anger, and readiness to use punishment reflect in my **attitude.** When they do something I judge to be "bad," I'd say (**self-talk**), "It's just like him or her to do that," and I reinforce the negative **behavior.** The kid thinks (self-talk), "Mom expects me to be a holy terror," and the kid becomes a holy terror! The kid doesn't want to disappoint me!

If, on the other hand, I believe my kids are precious gifts to be loved and enjoyed, I reinforce the positive behavior. When they do something "bad", I take the time to help correct the behavior, and clarify my expectations for better conduct. Again, the kid doesn't want to disappoint me!

1. **Beliefs.** You can talk yourself into your beliefs—your truths. Your unconscious, unable to distinguish between fact and non-fact, believes whatever you tell it and then, does anything and everything it can to make your truth come true. Keep an eye on your beliefs—write them out as you realize them. Then ask yourself: Do you want them to come true? Do they enhance your life? Your beliefs create your expectations.

2. **Expectations.** Once you believe something firmly, you gauge your expectations to fit your belief. Expectations are the most powerful forces in human relations. People will try to live up to expectations—their own, and those of others. Impossible expectations are among the most damaging forces there are; your child can never measure up to your yardstick of expectations. You are constantly disappointed and your child is constantly discouraged. Your child doesn't see that the expectation is unrealistic, but concludes, "I'm inadequate; something's wrong with me." Likewise, if you expect too little of your children, they will conclude that you don't believe in them; they probably won't make an effort. With unrealistic expectations, everyone's self-esteem suffers. Your expectations create your attitudes.

3. **Attitudes.** Attitudes are habits of thought. At first we form habits; then our habits form us. Attitudes of respect or disrespect, trust or distrust, encouragement or discouragement,

optimism or pessimism color our every day judgments.

4. **Judgment.** Often we make judgments based on out-dated beliefs, unrealistic expectations, or unforgiving attitudes. We judge others based on their jobs, their taste in clothing, and the expressions on their faces. We also judge people—usually unfairly—on their sex and their race. If we let our judgments get in the way (as judgments tend to do), we find ourselves dealing with our own beliefs—and not with another human being. If we form our judgments before interacting with someone—if we pre-judge—this becomes prejudice. When we feel the need to judge others from our own insecurity, we need to boost our own self-esteem instead (See Chapter 3). We can become aware of our judgments by listening to our self-talk.

5. **Self-Talk.** Words have great creative power; they can enhance or damage our self-esteem and the self-esteem of others. Our beliefs are enforced and repeated all the time in our thoughts with words. This is called self-talk. Self-talk, whether positive or negative, leads to behavior.

6. **Behavior.** We behave as if our beliefs are true. Our reality, the truth which we live, is a result of our beliefs. In order to change our behavior or that of our kids, therefore, we need to explore the beliefs that underpin the system. To change behaviors we must change the understanding that stands under them. Otherwise, behaviors will continue to reinforce beliefs that don't work any more.

One of the best ways to make things happen is to believe that it is so. "As you believe," taught Jesus, "so shall it be done unto you." For example, one-fourth to one-third of patients show improvement when given placebos by their physicians. Even though the pill has no active ingredients, it is powerful because the patients trust the physicians, and believe they are being cured.

People have a variety of beliefs about life—for example, Life is a bowl of cherries, or life is the pits. Life is to be enjoyed—or endured. You can't have everything, or you can have it all. Some beliefs are life enhancing. Others create limitations, pain, and havoc in our lives.

We look for things that prove we're right, that fit and validate our beliefs. It's called selective perception. If I believe that kids are bad, I look for things that prove I'm right. And whatever I look for, I find. In focusing on the negative, I filter out all the fun and delightful things they do. When they are helpful and do cute things, I say, "That's not like you," because it doesn't fit what I believe about them. When their behavior fits my belief, I say, "That's just like you." So for better or worse, I keep reinforcing the behavior that proves that I'm right. Kids repeat the behavior that we reinforce and expect. They become what we believe that they are. *What we believe is what we get.*

But rather than changing our expectations, too often we find that *we would rather be right than happy.* For example, Dad might say to Jack, "You're no good, just like your Uncle Harry." The label creates a negative expectation that Jack wants to "live up to." A self-fulfilling prophecy, Jack will tend to become like his uncle. Dad feels smug because he was "right" about the kid. Yet Jack thinks he's no good, Dad is disappointed, and everyone is miserable. Or, a mother might believe that her child did something bad; believing this she "knows it" and may act on it *even if it's not so.*

Examine your other beliefs. What do you believe about yourself? If you know that you're valuable and competent, you expect positive relationships and achievements. Self-esteem is believing that you are a worthwhile person. The higher your self-esteem, the higher your expectations (short of expecting "perfection"). If you believe that you are the scum of the earth, you'll expect very little of (and for) yourself. The lower your self-esteem, the lower your expectations. And *you get in life what you believe you deserve.*

When something isn't working in their lives, seldom do people search for the real source of the problem and unravel the underlying cause. Yet this is what we must do with the beliefs that limit our lives and harm our relationships. We must examine the hand-me-down beliefs, keep only those that enhance our lives and our families, ridding ourselves of the ones that are damaging to ourselves and others. Our beliefs are too powerful to be ignored; our truths and a better reality depend on making some conscious choices about them.

18.

Self-Talk

I used to stalk wild asparagus in the spring. Equipped with a pillow-case and a tiny pocket knife, I set out every four or five days looking for new shoots. One beautiful day, I discovered some luscious stalks just begging to be picked—on the wrong side of a barbed wire fence. I tried to resist the temptation but....

While harvesting my new asparagus patch, I became aware of someone approaching me. Turning, I saw an older man with a little brown bag—and a great big butcher knife! I stood, smiled weakly, and gulped. The man mumbled something about "territory," making me a little nervous. Trying to change the subject, I introduced myself and asked him to tell me about himself. Mr. Miller had grown up there, and as a kid he used to ice skate for miles on the frozen ditch. He'd never married and lived alone at the edge of town. In an effort to make a graceful exit before he could bring up territory again, I invited him to join my family for a steak and asparagus dinner. He smiled and said, "Much obliged, ma'am, but I don't mix well."

His words echoed in my mind as I walked home. He had probably said "I don't mix well" thousands, if not millions, of times throughout his life—to himself and to others. He had let me in on some of his self-talk. And of course, he didn't show up for dinner.

Mr. Miller sees himself as shy—perhaps as a social misfit. This ties in to his self-talk, his feelings and his behavior. The whole behavior pattern may have begun years ago. Perhaps he overheard an off-hand remark from a significant person. Or perhaps he was told over and over as a child that he was clumsy and stupid, and learned to believe that people wouldn't like him if he tried to "mix".

Our *self-talk* reflects our beliefs and creates our *feelings*. We express our feelings through our *behavior* which reinforces our *self-concept*.

If you repeated "I don't mix well" over and over to yourself, what would you feel? Lonely, lacking in confidence, low in self-esteem?

How would you behave? Might you be awkward, withdrawing, isolated? Self-talk is self-fulfilling. It reflects our self-concept or beliefs about ourselves and about life; it creates feelings which we express through our behavior. Finally, our behavior reinforces our self-concept.

Self-concept. Self-concept is simply the belief or picture you have of yourself at any given moment. It changes as you change. Many people have a mistaken idea of self-concept. Janet might say, "I was shy when I was born, I'm shy today, and I'll be shy the day I die." Janet is stuck.

Self-image is how you imagine yourself: what you can be and how others see you. Your self-image determines your performance. A negative self-image automatically sets up a failure mechanism. A positive self-image sets up a success mechanism.

Self-talk. We talk to ourselves all the time. Self-talk refers to the most important and powerful inner voice that we hear in our thoughts or beneath them. It controls our beliefs, our self-image, our self-concept, and, of course, our self-esteem.

One winter when I was skiing, for example, I fell every time the trail was steep. I noticed that just before I fell, I'd say, "I'm going to fall." I decided to flip my self-talk and said, "I'm doing great!" That affirmation encouraged me and changed my attitude. I maneuvered down the hill like a pro.

Self-talk prescribes our self-esteem. With our self-talk, we plant in our unconscious what will grow in our lives. We either encourage or discourage ourselves; we lift ourselves up or put ourselves down. The quality of self-talk determines whether we are our own best friend or worst enemy. Only when we tune in and listen to the old messages from the past can we begin to free ourselves of their grip on our present life.

Remember the slogan we heard when computers first appeared: "Garbage in, garbage out." (GIGO) If you were to bake a gingerbread cake with ingredients such as dust, mustard, and small sharp nails, it wouldn't come out of the oven smelling warm and spicy and wonderful like gingerbread should. Likewise, if a lot ot garbage has found its way into your mind, it probably spills negativity into your life.

When your self-esteem drops, listen to what you're saying to yourself. The reason most people have low self-esteem is that they keep telling themselves how awful they are. People who were blamed and criticized a lot as children tend to replay those negative statements —"stinkin' thinking"— over and over again, as if they were endlessly looping cassette tapes. Often, the volume of the internal dialogue is so low that people aren't aware of it. Turn up the volume. What do you hear? Write it down. Do you like what you hear? What would you do if someone else said those things to you?

Once you know what you say to yourself, you are free to make changes. *With awareness comes choice.* You can continue to repeat those messages, or make a new tape.

Feelings. Our self-talk, for better or worse, affects our feelings. Imagine yourself saying over and over, "I'm a loser." As you worry that you might fail, you create feelings of failure: discouragement, defeat, and depression. You keep yourself from taking any risks whatsoever. You stagnate. Now, let that go. Say to yourself several times instead, "I'm a winner." Your thoughts about winning and succeeding create winning feelings: encouragement, motivation, and excitement. You can use those feelings to confront the negative ones, and you'll find you have less fear of expressing your desires and intentions.

Behavior. We tend to act out feelings—with words and/or behavior. If we feel like winners, we act like winners—working hard, thinking clearly, and doing what we need to do to win. If we feel like losers, we act like losers and become losers. Our behaviors reinforce our self-concept—seeing ourselves as either winners or losers. Over time, we tend to become what we think about the most.

I remember a woman who cried herself to sleep every night because she thought she was a "bad" mother. That thought created feelings (guilt, sadness, and anger), that led to behavior (crying every night), that affected her self-concept—and her ability to be with her child. Instead of beating herself up, she could change her self-talk. Instead of discouraging herself, she could substitute encouraging affirmations instead. She might say, "I, _____, am a loving and effective mother" twenty or thirty times each day. It may feel like a lie, at first, but would get easier and more believable. The positive self-talk would alter her feelings about herself, and her behavior and self-concept would reflect the difference.

We can give ourselves messages that reinforce the negative—or that affirm the positive in our lives and help bring it about. Affirmations empower us to change our thinking—and our lives.

115

"Stinkin' Thinking"

There are some patterns of "stinkin' thinking" that we all share—games we play with our minds that keep us stuck in a win-lose mindset. We need to learn to catch ourselves in the act with these faulty habits, and laugh at our assumptions.

• In **polarized (either-or) thinking**[1], there is no gray area, no middle ground. You are either good or bad, perfect or a failure. As a result, emotions swing dramatically from one extreme to the other. Because of one little flaw, you become totally worthless.

The Alternative: Watch for either-or, black-white judgments. When you catch yourself doing that, ask how the opposite is also true. If, for example, you hear yourself saying, "The house is a total mess," look for parts of the house that are not messy. Realize that, with your 1 or 10 thinking, you block out 2 through 9. Lower your expectations and look for the gray areas that make up most of our experience.

• In **personalization**, we take everything personally, even when it isn't personal. For example, I might see someone scowling and conclude that she is scowling at me. At dinner, if I make broccoli and someone doesn't like it, I might conclude that something's wrong with me, and feel hurt.

The Alternative: If it isn't personal, don't take it personally. Check out your assumptions. Ask questions. Maybe they had a bad experience with broccoli once! Maybe she always scowls! Detach yourself from the situation for a moment: it most likely has nothing to do with you or your personal worth. If a kid makes a mess, and Mother says, "How could you do that to me?"—maybe she should consider the more likely possibility: the kid made the mess for himself or herself, without a thought of hurting Mother. Parents need to separate themselves from their children so they don't take kids' behavior personally. The higher our own self-esteem and the more we learn, the easier it is to not hook in to such things.

• In **projection,** or mindreading, we project on to others what is going on in our own self-talk. Did you ever wear a shirt with a spot on it and imagine that everyone you spoke to was staring at it critically? Have you ever been sure that the reason a friend hasn't called (or written) is because they were mad at you—when they weren't? Or have you been in an argument with a friend or lover, and accused him or her of the very things you discovered yourself feeling—five minutes later?

The Alternative: When you catch yourself projecting your thoughts, do a reality check. If your self-talk thinks your friend is judging you on your messy house, try to prove it. Is she eyeing everything critically? Is she wearing white gloves? Or is she looking right at you smiling—happy to see you? Chances are it's a fabrication of your own faulty thinking. Your negative feelings (guilt, anger, rejection) may be the result of your own thinking (self-talk) and have nothing to do with your visitor. And listen carefully to the words that come out of your mouth. They may hold a message for you.

• With **catastrophizing** we imagine and expect the worst. A headache is a sure sign of a brain tumor; a minor financial setback means you'll starve to death, for sure. Any little thing may be a sign of impending doom. These days, of course, it's easy to do, as the news brings us new reasons to panic every day; with catastrophizing, we can put ourselves into a total panic that devastates our sense of well-being.

The Alternative: Mark Twain remarked, "I've had many worries in my life, and most of them never came to pass." Consider the odds against your conclusion—the brain tumor, starvation. Don't make a mountain out of a molehill. Think of the many times you imagined the worst and were wrong. Do you want to keep doing it? Disaster is always a remote possibility, but never very probable. Trust life and remember the saying, "God never gives us more than we can handle."

• In **blaming** we find fault either in ourselves or in others. We either assume total responsibility for everything that goes wrong ("What's wrong with me?") or we accept no personal responsibility for difficulties and put it all on others. We either point a blaming finger at everyone else or beat our breast in guilt.

The Alternative: We are all responsible for our behavior and the consequences of it. In relationships, both persons are responsible for creating the problem—and for creating a solution. Listen for the words "blame" and "fault." Get rid of them. Instead, think in terms of accepting responsibility—and sharing it. Only then can you move ahead—and either solve problems, or forgive them.

• With **overgeneralization,** if something bad happened to you once, you expect it to happen again. Limited situations lead to absolute conclusions. You make one mistake, like botching an important test in junior high, and you conclude that you're no good at math. Someone else makes a mistake, and you totally reject them. When visiting a new relative years ago, I discovered that there was no toilet paper on the bathroom roll. I concluded that moment that she was an awful housewife. If you notice that one thing is wrong, and another thing, you leap to the conclusion that everything is wrong—all the time. You may even talk yourself into believing that it's bad now, it always was, and it always will be—forever and ever, amen.

The Alternative: First of all, be aware of what you are doing. When you notice it, examine the evidence for your conclusion and then the evidence against it. Weigh your information. (It took me a long time to realize what a precious contribution that "lousy housewife" made to the family—t.p. or no. Her gifts, instead, were of laughter and fishing and sauerkraut chocolate cake.) (Makes it moist....) Also, listen for those "big" words: never, always, everybody, nobody. Use them only with great care, or when you're joking.

• **Having to be right** all the time puts you into conflict with everyone whose viewpoint differs. It makes people hard of hearing. When others differ from you, you ignore them or have to prove them wrong. You find yourself in more power struggles than you'd like. Minor differences seem major because self-esteem and personal worth are at stake. When reality differs from the way you think it should be, you deny it. Having to be right all the time makes people lonely.

The Alternative: Reality is not the way we want it to be—but the way it is. We need to remove the blinders and see what really is, instead of trying to force the world to fit our personal image of how it's supposed to be. In our world we have many different people with different perceptions, experiences, and styles. There are many different "right" ways. It would be a dull world if there were only one right way. And whose right way would be accepted as right by everyone else? (If it weren't yours... could you be happy?) We must each find what's best for ourselves—what is right—and allow others to do the same.

Affirmations

I'd like to ask you to pause and do a little fantasy. Imagine, for a minute, a blue hippo. Then: *don't* think of a blue hippo!

How did you get rid of the blue hippo? You probably thought of something else—maybe a red hippo or a green giraffe or a flower. To get rid of the first image, most people replace it with another. And that is exactly how we must work with our unconscious to make important changes in our lives. *Think about—affirm—what you want in order to get rid of what you don't want.*

With affirmations we talk back to negative self talk. We reprogram ourselves and create the kind of transformation we felt when we learned to ride a bicycle or swim. We can move from "I can't" to "Of course I can!" We no longer have to be controlled by our past. Affirmations help us believe in the good things we want and expect for ourselves. We can substitute positive messages to expel the garbage from our minds and to heal the damage caused by years of negative thinking.

We can also use affirmations to counter put-downs. When someone tells eleven year old Frank that he's stupid, he corrects it in his self-talk saying, "That's not true. I'm good at math."

I'd like to invite you to do another fantasy. Close your eyes and imagine someone very special entering the room, walking up behind you, gently touching your shoulders, and whispering something important about you that you've been wanting to hear. Listen.

Those whispered words may be the perfect affirmation for you. Rephrase them in the form, "I, _____, am _____." You can be your own best friend and give this message to yourself instead of hoping and wishing for someone else to say it to you. Every morning when you look in the mirror you can say, "I accept and love you just the way you are." You can also say: "I am now creating my life exactly as I want it." Repeat such affirmations twenty to thirty times every day, allowing the positive feelings little by little, until you believe yourself, until you become yourself.

This process makes more sense once you understand the nature of the unconscious: it can't tell the difference between fact and nonfact, between what's imagined and what's real. Your unconscious will believe anything you tell it and will do everything to make that happen. As with a fertile garden, whatever you plant in your unconscious will grow. If you plant carrots, you won't get petunias; and if you plant nothing, you'll probably get weeds.

What are the seeds for the unconscious? The thoughts we think (self-talk) and the pictures we imagine. "Imagination is everything," said Albert Einstein. "It is the preview of life's coming attractions." What we see is what we get. Also, the words we repeat over and over in our minds have great power; eventually they become our reality. *We become what we think about the most.*

If your children tell you that they can't do something, help them turn it around saying, "Let's pretend that you can!" And be sure to read that wonderful story, *The Little Engine That Could.* That little engine knew how to use affirmations to achieve greatness.

A child with positive self-talk and high self-esteem is a child who will have positive behavior that reinforces the positive self-talk. On the other hand, a child with a negative self-talk and low self-esteem will exhibit negative behavior that reinforces the negative self-talk. Whatever you can do to build your child's self-esteem will pay off in a happier child with more positive behaviors.

You can direct your thoughts. When you accept responsibility for your self-talk you take charge of your self-esteem. *By changing your mind, you can change your life.*

19.

Obsession With Perfection

"There is no perfectionism. It's really the world's greatest con game. it promises richness and delivers misery."
—David Burns, M.D.[1]

I had to be a perfect hostess. I had to cook a perfect meal and set a perfect table with no wrinkles in the tablecloth. The house had to be perfect. And when the doorbell rang, I had to be calm and smiling as though I'd done nothing all day long. The stress and anxiety kept me from enjoying myself or my guests. I was a perfectionist.

When I realized how much my perfectionist expectations were inhibiting my lifestyle and cramping my self-expression, I decided to make some major changes. Now, as a recovering perfectionist, I am free to attempt new things and enjoy myself more. I've taken more risks, made more mistakes, and gained wisdom. I have become a professional speaker and have written a successful book. Mostly out of the clutches of perfectionism, life is much more fun and a lot easier.

Many children conclude that only if they are perfect will their parents love them. Having to earn acceptance and love, they work harder and harder to be accepted, to be loved, to be okay. The ultimate hope of this ongoing struggle is that Mom and Dad might accept, approve, and love them unconditionally—just for being themselves.

The media, Hollywood, and magazines bombard all of us, women in particular, with expectations of perfection. Striving to become a perfect wife with a Jane Fonda body, a perfect mother with honor role children, and a Julia Child cook serving gourmet dinners sets one up for chronic disappointment, dissatisfaction and exhaustion. Only if we are perfect do we think we are okay. The cultural pressures are so pervasive, it's hard to escape them.

Always looking for something wrong, perfectionists find it, then are shocked and angry about it. They have unrealistic or impossible expectations: only perfection will do. Yet, human beings can't be perfect for very long. Just one failing, fault, or flaw proves what perfectionists believe deep down—that they are total failures. This either/or thinking—I am a 10 or I am a zero—allows no middle ground. I am either all good or all bad. Mistakes, therefore, are terrifying. The gray area—1 through 9—is missing. One perfectionist learned clearly from her mother, "You are perfect or you are nothing."

They have difficulty accepting themselves, therefore they have difficulty accepting others. Judgmental and critical of themselves, they tend to be judgmental and critical of others. Yet, while good at giving criticism, they fear it from others and easily become defensive. They fight to be right because they can't stand the thought of being wrong, resulting in conflicts in family and professional relationships. Under pressure to be perfect, they pretend and cover up to keep up a façade of perfection. Playing this role while knowing that it's phoney creates absolute stress and can tear them up inside.

Decision-making produces intense anxiety because they want to make a perfect decision. They may procrastinate in doing tasks, or avoid finishing them; if they don't start or don't finish, they can avoid being judged. Perfectionists take great pains—then give them to others. In business settings they waste immeasurable amounts of time and materials at high costs to the company; they can spend hours writing one letter.

Many children feel the pressure to be perfect. Getting up to bat can be terrifying when you believe that you have to hit the ball every time it crosses the plate. The tension is intensified if a perfectionist parent is watching. Kids might quit or they may not even bother to try. If they don't try, they reason, they can't fail.

The thought of making their bed or cleaning their bedroom can strike them with terror, discouragement, and despair. One thirteen-year-old boy, after spending many hours cleaning his room called his dad to inspect it. Dad glanced around the room, stroked the wall saying, "You didn't oil the paneling." Everyone around a perfectionist suffers from low self-esteem.

Perfectionists may end up doing all the work themselves because no one else can do it "just right", which means perfect. They suffer, therefore, from chronic fatigue and stress. When they do successfully complete a task, they never give themselves a pat on the back because they are busy looking for flaws. A perfectionist , for example, who raises $50,000 for his or her favorite charity might say, "It should have been $75,000." They don't see the success and savor it; they only see how it wasn't good enough.

Child perfectionists with straight As have killed themselves when they received their first B. A similar story is that of Ludwig Boltzmann, considered to be one of the twenty greatest physicists of all time.   Acclaimed as one of the principal founders of statistical mechanics, he, himself, was never quite satisfied with his work and took his life. His perfectionist perceptions prevented him from feeling content with his outstanding achievements. Perfectionism can be deadly, psychologically and physically.

Perfectionists focus on surface qualities. They work to develop a perfect façade based on an image/ideal/fantasy of how they think they (and others) are "supposed to" be. A pimple, a spot on the shirt, unruly hair command their attention to such a degree that they may not hear what the kid is telling them. They may miss their child's feelings, concerns, struggles, growth, and the inner beauty. Perfectionists may be stunted in their development due to confusion and anxiety, lack of appreciation and support.

No human being is perfect. There is no such thing as a "perfect man," a "perfect woman," a "perfect child," a "perfect couple," or a "perfect body." "Perfect" media models may have endured cosmetic surgery to alter nose, chin, or breasts. If all else fails to remove or cover-up wrinkles, moles, pimples, and grey hair, the photographs are air-brushed to remove every last flaw. We compare ourselves to the manufactured pictures of models and then think that something's wrong with us. (See Chapter 20.)

Of the thousands of participants in my workshops striving to be perfect, no one has achieved it. All their lives they've worked so that one day they would be really okay which, to a perfectionist, means perfect.

It's no fun being a perfectionist. Joy is missing. Playful abandon, utter relaxation and joys are absent.   Spontaneity is rare. Perfectionism is a compulsion that may predispose people to alcoholism, eating disorders and other obsessive-compulsive behaviors.

How does one recover from perfectionism? Here are seven tips.

• **Admit that you're only human.** It is our privilege as human beings to be imperfect! Some even say it's our duty. Turkish carpet makers are known to weave flaws into their design with the reasoning that only God is perfect! In this culture, it takes courage to allow ourselves to be imperfect. Yet, when we accept our imperfections and forgive ourselves, we are able to accept and forgive others.

Who said that parents always had to be right? When you accept yourself completely—including the fact that you are fallible—the burden lightens. It's a relief not to have to be perfect—not to have to play God.

Admit your mistakes. You can simply state "Yesterday I said (or did) such-and-such and I realize today that I was wrong." Kids know how human they are; when you share your flaws with them, it gives them more hope—and builds a bond between you.

• **Turn mistakes into teachers.** If it is human to err, then children are very human. They are always losing, forgetting, or spilling things. Don't cry over spilled milk, just clean it up and be more careful next time. Self-esteem sags when they make mistakes; when they fix them, they regain their self-esteem. Help them to figure out what happened so they can avoid a repeat performance. A mistake, after all, is just one way that didn't work.

A friend of mine went through a series of unhealthy relationships before noticing that she was making the same moves each time with the same type of man. As soon as she realized this, her "luck" began to change, and she suddenly met a man with whom she could be herself.

In doing, risking, and trying new things, we develop judgment skills. We learn how to evaluate, how to analyze, how to determine what old information transfers to new situations. A person who has made mistakes has gained wisdom.

It can be difficult for parents to watch their kids struggle as a result of their mistakes. The impulse to protect and rescue them is very strong. Don't, however, rescue them from their mistakes unless they are in danger. Actions have consequences, and if they are rescued before they have the chance to discover this for themselves, they don't learn the lessons.

Ideally, children will learn from their little mistakes early in life when they're around people who love and can guide them. As they get older and the stakes get higher, mistakes can be dangerous, even lethal. Viewing mistakes as learning opportunities is a life-saving and life-enhancing skill. When they learn from mistakes, they gain confidence, competence, and judgment skills.

• **Laugh at your mistakes.** Share them with family and friends. One mom told me that they play Bloopers at the dinner table. Mom and Dad begin with stories of their daily blunders, and each kid follows.

After filling my gas tank one time, for example, I went through the car wash. It was only when I turned onto the street and heard a clunk did I realize that I had not put the gas cap back on. I spent the rest of the afternoon with my mechanic trying to figure out how to get rid of the soapy water without sacrificing the tank of gas. At home, everyone laughed at my mistake. My kids learned from it and will never repeat it—nor will I.

Blooper time is a fun time since the whole family has a chance to laugh with each other, at each other, and at themselves—and then get on with life. Modeling this to our children is a wonderful gift to them. It lightens up life for everyone in the family.

• **Reorder your priorities.** One mother of three preschool children vacuumed the carpet three times each day. I suggested that she rethink this. The following week she reported to the class that she had cut back to twice a day. "No one seemed to notice," she said, "and I had more time for my children." Do you want to be a slave to household perfection? A perfect house is impossible with children. Lower your expectations. Stop trying to be Superwoman or Superman. "Simplify, simplify, simplify," wrote Henry David Thoreau. Create an easier lifestyle for yourself. Design a family life that is healthier and enjoyable for all of you.

Life is short; examine your priorities. What's really important in your life? Good parenting? Go for excellence in that area. Be the best that you can be! In other areas, planting a garden, for example, "good enough" will do just fine. Beet seeds do not have to be in a straight line exactly 1/2 inch deep and 1/2 inch apart. Do you really want to spend three days getting the beet seeds in just right?

• **Stop the stinkin' thinking that says "I'm not good enough."** Listen to whose voice it is that tells you that. Then realize that that was *only their opinion* at that moment in time based on *their* perfectionist expectations. The fact is, *you are good enough and always have been!* Change the nagging, damaging message that keeps telling you differently. Tell yourself, "I, [your name], am good enough." Repeat this a few times. It may feel strange at first but that will change. Over time, this affirmation will heal you and help you to transcend perfectionism.

• **Be gentle with yourself.** It's fine to want to have a nice table set for a dinner party, but spending an hour folding and re-folding napkins, ironing and re-ironing the tablecloth is problematic. Relax. Breathe deeply. Be flexible. Focus on and enjoy the experience of life rather than the accomplishment of it.

• **Put more spontaneity, silliness, and joy into your life.** Kids can teach you how to play. If you don't have any, borrow some. When you pick up your child from day care, stop at a park to unwind and reconnect. Roll down a grassy hill, go down a slide, skip rope. Pretend. They can help you make a fool of yourself and it might be the best thing for you. When you laugh and play together, stress goes down and self-esteem goes up. As you create rich memories, you'll nudge yourself beyond the obsession with perfection.

You can't be a friend unless you are your self.
You can't be your self unless you know your self.
You can't know your self unless you admit your mistakes.
You can't admit your mistakes if you're pretending to be perfect.
And you can't be perfect — because you're human.
Enjoy it! Celebrate it!

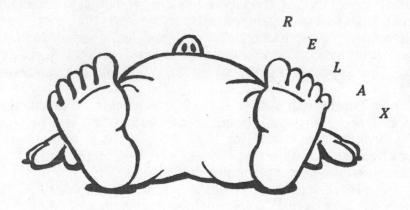

R
E
L
A
X

20.

Cultural Barriers to Self-Esteem

*"The first problem for all of us, men and women,
is not to learn, but to unlearn."*

—Gloria Steinem[1]

Self-esteem is as important to our well-being as legs are to a table. It is essential for physical and mental health and for happiness. Given its importance, everyone should be taught skills for self-esteem development. Instead, we are more often taught ideas and behaviors that lower self-esteem—our own and that of our children.

Young children have wonderful memories. By nature, they are very impressionable because they have so much to learn to prepare themselves for the rest of life. Ready and eager to learn about their world and how to be in it, they take in everything. Naturally trusting, they believe what they are taught, accepting it as the "truth" about how the world is. The "truth" that they learn shapes their behavior.

In simpler cultures this works very well. From parents and others who care about them, children learn what they need to know in order to become effective adults. In our culture things are different; children learn less from their preoccupied parents, little from caring neighbors, and too much from Hollywood and Madison Avenue. As a result, they miss out on the essential lifeskills they need to become healthy and competent adults. Our mass-media cultural myths and values clutter their minds—and ours—with misinformation that can be a prison of frustration, dissatisfaction, alienation, and pain.

From an unhealthy society and dysfunctional families, children learn dysfunctional patterns of relating to others. Co-dependency, occurring in about 98% of the adult population, is responsible for most human misery according to authors Barry and Janae Weinhold. "Co-dependency is learned dysfunctional behavior and is the result of the failure to complete one or more of the important developmental tasks during early childhood."[2]

Some major symptoms of co-dependency are

- Low self-esteem
- Being a people-pleaser and approval seeker
- Feeling like a martyr
- Having poorly defined psychological boundaries
- Seeking outside stimulation (alcohol, food, work, or sex, for example) as a distraction from feelings
- Feeling "addicted" to and trapped in damaging relationships, and powerless to change them.
- Inability to express love and true intimacy

Any one of these characteristics can create problems for individuals. Combined with others, they create a trap for parents and children alike. Recovery comes with unraveling what doesn't work, and replacing it with what does work.

It takes courage and a lot of time to begin to find one's own set of beliefs and values. I spent many years sifting through what I had learned early in my life, unraveling the misinformation, poking holes in my myths, peeling off the layers of my beliefs. I had to unlearn what didn't work, then relearn what did. At age forty, I felt that I finally knew what I needed to know at fourteen.

Perfectionism is an extremely common stumbling block to self-esteem. This chapter lists many related barriers to self-esteem and mental health that our culture constructs. Because western civilization has long been influenced by patriarchal values, many of them apply more to women than to men. These barriers can be deadly—either psychologically (draining our life force), or physically (resulting in illness and suicide), but they *can* be overcome with awareness, attention, new choices, and some work. What we find on the other side of these barriers is an easier, more fulfilling life.

Self Put-Downs

In high school, I once told a friend that I thought I had a nice smile, and she thought that I was conceited and shouldn't toot my own horn. I had a little talk with myself and concluded that it's not okay to say good things about myself in this world. Later on, if I would have had the nerve to again mention my smile, I'd say, "I have a nice smile—but I have lots of cavities."

Many people, women in particular, learned that it is not okay to say good things about themselves. When they did, they were criticized for bragging. So they learned to put themselves down instead. Doing that, their self-esteem suffered.

But Will Rogers said, "If it's the truth, it can't be bragging." No one achieves greatness by being self-deprecating—by putting themselves down. Scientists and soccer players, mothers and musicians, become great by acknowledging their strengths, believing in themselves, and by working hard for their personal goals. After setting a goal, they find encouragement and support from others, and take pride in their progress.

The word pride is used both positively—"I'm proud of you"—and negatively—"Don't be proud." To me, to be proud means to feel good about someone and/or their performance. On the other hand, to put yourself up and others down—"I'm great and you're not"—is false pride or egotism. Feeling good at someone's expense is not healthy.

Listen to what you say to yourself. Look into a mirror and tune in to your self-talk. Are you saying, "Boy, are *you* ugly/fat/dumb!" If a friend talked to you like that, how would you feel? Instead, say something nice to yourself. Whisper "sweet nothings" in your own ear. And tell other people the good things about yourself. Most people really *do* prefer to hear the positive things about you and your life rather than the negative things.

Begin also to listen closely to how you talk to your children. Listen for, then ban negativity; it lowers self-esteem. Look for the good intentions in stupid behavior, and acknowledge them. Catch your kids being good and appreciate them. This will make them more aware of their positive attributes and raise their self-esteem. Being positive is also more fun than being negative!

Listen to how your children talk about themselves. Negative statements, such as "I'm so dumb" or "I never do anything right," let you know what they are repeating over and over again to themselves. The negative self-talk leads to negative feelings and negative behavior.

To counter this, you might introduce the Eleventh Commandment: "Thou shalt not speak negatively of thyself or others." Establish a rule that every negative statement about oneself is to be countered with a positive statement. This will help you become aware of how you talk to yourself—and about others—and will flip the focus to the positive.

Look for the good qualities in yourself and in your kids. Ask them to tell you what they like about themselves. Sit down with them and encourage them to talk about how they're special. Get them to start learning to think positively about themselves. Parents and teachers alike report that kids love doing this, and their self-esteem increases instantly.

Self-Sacrifice

In the tradition of our culture, the role of "woman" somehow became identified as caretaker of everyone's needs but their own. Women have learned to expect and hope that by doing enough taking care of others, their turn would come automatically; but somehow, it rarely does. Women are still led to believe that taking care of themselves is "selfish." (Jewish mothers get the stereotype for this, but we all do it!) "I almost denied myself out of existence," confessed one woman who was taught to be self-negating. Many became longsuffering martyrs and doormats, watching life pass them by. Many burned out.

Those who never stand up for their own preferences or rights, however, can be annoying. A classic example is that of a friend's grandmother who was invited to tour San Francisco in a convertible. If she sat in the passenger's seat, she could enjoy the view without too much wind, and the older kids in the back could enjoy a windy, gorgeous ride. She refused to take the front seat, though, insisting she was being treated too well. Consequently, the top had to stay up. She couldn't appreciate the exciting views, and no one had a good time. By taking the back seat and trying not to inconvenience anyone, she inconvenienced everyone.

After having two babies eleven months apart, I wish someone had told me to take care of myself and get plenty of exercise and rest. I wish someone had given me permission to play more. I wish someone had told me that nap time for baby is "self-time" for mom. Mothers have to take care of themselves so they can take care of others. Self-care is the primary issue because you can't give what you haven't got.

The last part of Jesus' only commandment states that we must love our neighbor as *ourself*. Self-love, therefore, comes first. The best thing you can do for your kids is to be good and loving to yourself. Take good care of yourself for your own sake and for theirs.

"Kids' needs are best met by grownups whose needs are met," writes Jean Illsley Clarke. Yet there are times when we need to put our own needs on hold, especially with young children. One of the challenges of parenting is to do for our kids *and* for ourselves. We need to strike a healthy balance in which no one comes out losing.

A large part of self-esteem comes from feeling that we deserve to be happy, to have fun, to enjoy life, to do the things we want to do. Here is a good exercise in self-nourishment. Pause for a moment and make a list of twenty things you love to do. Be aware, as you are writing, of when you last did those things. Then cross off any that are not good for you.

Your homework: Every day do at least one of those things for yourself. When you are good to yourself, you feel good about yourself. This is called self-care. Your intention is important. Most people like to take a hot bath. If you do it because you deserve a treat, the bath will do more than cleanse you—it will also enhance your self-esteem.

It's okay and necessary to relax, and to take time for yourself. It's also important to take time for your friends, for your spouse. You entered a relationship to be friends, to be lovers, to have fun together. Often, when kids come along, parents fall out of touch with each other. It's important to nurture and enrich your relationship with your mate; that's where it all started. And one day, when your kids are grown, you will be back to being alone with each other. The love that exists between parents showers down on the children. Being in the presence of two people who truly love and support each other has a powerful positive effect on children. All important relationships need to be nurtured.

Always Pleasing Others

Many people are taught to spend their lives trying to please others. They never say no, for fear of displeasing someone or making someone mad at them. Because they were raised seeking acceptance, they became people pleasers, begging for crumbs of approval from others. They smile all the time, hoping that everyone will like them and enjoy being with them. These people never feel really okay; they suffer from low self-esteem.

Here's a message for people pleasers: the person most important for you to please is yourself. Think of a time you prepared a nice meal for someone and worked hard on it, but something wasn't quite right. Afterward, someone gave you a compliment—"That was delicious!" What did you do with their remark? Not being pleased yourself, you probably discounted it or ignored it because you didn't believe it. In fact, if the whole world had stood up and thanked you, and you were not pleased yourself, you probably would not have noticed the applause! You must first be pleased before you can let in the appreciation and recognition of others. Then, if someone does give you a compliment, it's like icing on a cake.

As a senior in high school, I was voted "the most cheerful" person in a class of three hundred girls. Wanting to be pleasing so that everyone would like me, I wore a permanent smile. It actually had little to do with cheer. I was shocked in graduate school to learn that statistically one out of eight people would not like me (or anyone else)!

Struggling with this, I learned that little girls are socialized to want to be liked by others, while boys are socialized to look for respect. I realized that, if being liked is most important, people will do anything to achieve it—even things against their principles. It's a vulnerable position, inviting manipulation (for example, "If you don't do_____, I won't like you"). People pleasers lack the inner strength to "just say no." Young girls, consequently, who want to be pleasing to others are easy victims of "date-rape."

After giving this lots of thought, I decided that I would rather have people respect me than like me. I stopped smiling all the time. I began to respect myself more, and others began to respect me more. My self-esteem moved up many notches as my definitions of what pleased *me* changed.

Assuming Too Much Responsibility for Other People's Lives

When babies are born, parents have total responsibility for their survival and well-being. As they grow and are able to do things for themselves, parents must turn over more and more responsibility to them—from feeding themselves to driving themselves—thereby lightening their own load.

If this transfer does not occur, if parents carry more responsibility than is necessary or appropriate, children are deprived of opportunities to grow, develop, and expand. If women believe that mothering is their only role, they may keep the responsibility of care-taking longer than necessary—and thus deprive their children of their own self-responsibility. Parents, carrying too much responsibility, may feel burdened and try to control others. Blame and anger often result with everyone's self-esteem dropping. Likewise, women often find themselves trying to "mother" their partners. Adults should be parents to children, not to other adults.

We can't remind ourselves often enough that every person is first and foremost responsible for himself or herself. The task of the parent shifts from having total responsibility over infants to having almost no responsibility over them as adults. The task of the child shifts from having no responsibility as an infant to having total responsibility as an adult. This gradual process, in harmony with the developmental stages of the child, occurs over fifteen to twenty years' time.

We all remember the delight of a youngster saying, "Look at me! I can do it all by myself!" We say, "Good for you! Now you can tie your own shoes." We can release some responsibility.

We teach children responsibility by teaching ourselves not to do things for them that they can do for themselves. And as they learn to do more and more things for themselves, their competence and confidence increase. As children assume more responsibility for their behavior and their lives, parents can relax their protectiveness, trust them more, and breathe a sigh of relief as their responsibility lightens. Then they can get on with other important areas of their lives.

Our Bodies are Never Okay

Most women think that something is wrong with their bodies. They compare themselves to the current "perfect" body type, put themselves down and feel bad. Like fashions, the ideal figure keeps shifting. The Playboy centerfold body, for example, is five pounds lighter than she was a few years ago. Perfect body types go in and out of style—yet our bodies stay basically the same.

The cultural stereotype for women's bodies is not only damaging, it is absurd. In her book, Jane Fonda discusses becoming bulimic in high school. "For several of us at my school," she writes, "it was the beginning of a nightmarish addiction that would undermine our lives for decades to come."[3] She, and many of us, became obsessed with an external ideal, and not the person inside.

Bulimia, anorexia, and other eating disorders have reached epidemic proportions. Little girls nine and ten years old are dieting because their mothers are—when they should be having a wonderful time climbing trees, riding bikes, and exploring the world. They have internalized the cultural value that they have to have a "perfect" (skinny) body in order to be okay; they are not okay as they are. Once, on a vacation in Puerto Vallarta, I did not wear my bathing suit to the beach. I compared myself to the other sun-worshipers and became self-conscious about my okay, but imperfect body; it embarrasses me to remember that. As women take in the cultural messages, many have learned to hate their bodies and reject themselves.

The obsession with physical perfection is not a personal problem, but a societal issue. Many women get discouraged and resort to drastic measures to match the current ideal figure, such as liposuction, tucks, rib removal, cosmetic surgery—in order to look "okay". Over one million American women have had breast enlargement operations creating a $300 million business for plastic surgeons. Aren't there more important things to spend money on than the illusion of perfection?

We come in all sizes, all shapes, all colors—and we are all okay. Understand that the cultural model is damaging and unhealthy. Your body is not an object—it's *you*. Accept your body. Love yourself just the way you are. If you want to make some changes, you will be more successful by being respectful and encouraging of yourself than by being rejecting and disgusted. Remember, *it's more important to be healthy than to be perfect.* If you care for yourself and enjoy living in your body, it will become your passport, not your prison. Your body has much to teach you; you can't have high self-esteem unless you love all of yourself—and that *includes* your beautiful thunder thighs!

Avoidance

Everyone has pain and discomfort at times. What do we learn to do with it?

- Deny. On our honeymoon, my husband and I agreed that *we* wouldn't have problems. This set us up for a relationship based on denial and gunnysacking.
- Distract. Occasionally a movie or a change of scenery can provide a needed break. Too many romance novels or soap operas, however, can be an addiction, an escape from life.
- Drug.[4] At home with three small children all day, a late afternoon glass of wine would help me survive the fatigue and calm the stress towards the end of the day. Yet this kept me from confronting and dealing with my problems for a long time.

Everyone uses strategies of avoidance at times. They can provide a brief vacation—a time for re-grouping. The danger lies in using these strategies as a matter of course—when denial, distraction, and drugs become a way to avoid dealing with life. When you avoid, you do nothing and nothing changes except, perhaps, your perceptions which may not be accurate.

Unfortunately, we live in a drug culture. Drugs that didn't exist a few years ago are now permanent crutches to those who have no better solutions to their troubles. We have a "war" on crack cocaine on the one hand, but there is as great an addiction to legal drugs, as well. For years, physicians have casually prescribed tranquilizers for unhappy people, instead of encouraging them to make changes in their lives. In 1960, Valium did not exist; now six billion tablets are consumed annually. The alcohol and tobacco industries spend millions advertising on television, magazines, and billboards, bombarding us with images of happiness through consumption of substances. Yet, these things do nothing for our self-esteem.

It takes more energy to avoid pain than to face it. When we avoid pain, we hold on to it. It becomes chronic. As long as we keep avoiding, we remain stuck in feelings of helplessness and numbness. We cut ourselves off from the compassion of understanding friends—and interrupt the process of healing. Sharing pain with others—as witnessed in funerals—allows an opening for giving and receiving support and for bonding.

Unhappy people and families don't become happy by pretending, denying, or avoiding reality. They become happy by talking, listening, negotiating, and making positive changes. They let go of self-defeating behavior that does not work.

In order for things to change, you must *do* something. You must attend to a flat tire—it does not fix itself. In figuring out how to solve the problem, you *do* something, you *change* something, and you *learn* something. When it's resolved, the pain is gone. You are stronger and feel the joy of overcoming. You were put on this earth not to struggle, but to grow.

Alcoholic Family Systems

Children of alcoholics are at the highest risk for physical, sexual, and emotional abuse, for neglect, and for other forms of violence and exploitation. In up to 90 percent of child abuse cases, alcohol is a significant factor. When parents are drunk or "high", they often do things they later regret. Alcoholism and other drug addictions devastate families. In addition to physical damage, children of alcoholics experience a wide range of psychological difficulties including learning disabilities, eating disorders, compulsive achieving, depression, shame, and guilt.

Adult children of alcoholics often have great difficulty with guilt, control, trust, denial of feelings, and intimacy. They are far more likely to become or marry alcoholics, and to suffer from relationship problems. Everyone's self-esteem and mental health is damaged.

An estimated 28 million Americans are children of alcoholics. They learn certain attitudes and behavior to survive. First and foremost, they learn to deny the problem. They also learn the rules: Don't talk. Don't trust. Don't feel. Those very skills that helped kids survive at home prevent them from thriving in life—from having healthy adult relationships.

Self-help groups are forming around the country for Adult Children of Alcoholics. These groups—and also AA groups, Al-anon and Ala-Teen groups—can help you understand the dynamics of alcoholic family systems. They can help you learn to become a loving parent to your own wounded inner child. They can help you deal with alcoholism, heal yourself, and prevent the disease from recurring in the next generation.

Patrick said, "Joining Adult Children of Alcoholics meetings has been the single most helpful and supportive thing I've done in my adult life. For the first time I understand why, for the past thirty-six years, I haven't felt good about myself, why I'm a caretaker and a perfectionist. It's such a relief to be in a room full of people who accept me as I am, who understand from the inside out what it's like, and to realize that I'm not bad, crazy, or sick—and that it's not hopeless. I've learned that it's okay to take care of myself and to like myself."

If your parents were alcoholic, it's not your fault. *You are not to blame*. You are not responsible for their problems. On the other hand, they may be responsible for some of yours. But *you* are responsible for the solution! Sort out in your mind what is yours and what is theirs.

Alcoholism is a family disease. *You hurt worst those you love the most.* If it runs in your family, break through the denial and deal with it—for your own sake, and for the sake of your children.

Dualistic Thinking

In this society, we have a tendency to see things in terms of opposites—black and white, rich and poor, heaven and hell, day and night. This wouldn't be so bad if we didn't also put value judgments on such pairs and label some things "good" and other things "bad". But because we think this way, we have to be careful of the language we use with our children.

Did you ever do something stupid? Of course. We all have. But does that mean that you *are* stupid? Of course not! *What you do is not who you are.*

Remember a time when, as a child, someone pointed a finger at you and yelled, "You're a bad boy" or "You're a bad girl." What did you feel? Did you feel it again just now? How old were you at the time? One woman stated, "I did a dumb little thing, and with those words my mother wiped me out. Yelling that I was a "bad girl" devastated me. I felt rejected, worthless, awful, and unlovable. Looking back, I realize that I wasn't a bad girl; I was a good girl who had made a dumb mistake."

Labels like "bad", "clumsy", and "stupid" can be more powerful than they are meant to be. Value judgments applied to a *person* can damage self-esteem for years to come. Adults who give "bad kid" messages probably do not understand the importance of separating the person from the behavior. In dealing with the unacceptable behavior, they reject the whole child, who feels wounded, worthless, and devastated.

It is possible to deal with unacceptable behavior without damaging anyone. *We must separate the person from the behavior.* Think about when you were a child. What was considered "bad" in your family. When did your parents and siblings use the word? In what context? After all your life experiences, what do you now consider to be "bad"? What do you want your children to think is "bad"?

Different parents apply that word to many diverse behaviors, such as being noisy, forgetting a chore, getting a low grade, preferring a certain hairstyle. Then they don't label the behavior "bad"; they label the whole child "bad" which is certainly unfair. The child is a good person who was, perhaps, just being forgetful, confused, or exercising poor judgment. Instead of getting a heavy value judgment along with rejection and punishment, he or she probably needs your understanding more than anything else.

When dealing with unacceptable behavior, do it privately. Treat children with respect and caring. Sit down with them; touch them supportively. *Love the doer even when you don't like the deed.* Talk about what happened. Imagine that you can hang the problem behavior on the wall so that both can separate from it and discuss it objectively. What happened? What were they thinking? What are they feeling? What did they learn? How can they fix it? With this strategy you can both begin to see the gray area between good and bad, and the problem can get resolved without the child feeling rejected.

If you must scold your children when their *behavior* is bad, be careful that you don't label your *children* "bad." When labeled bad, they feel bad and behave badly—a self-fulfilling prophecy. They are good kids who may, at times, make mistakes or do dumb things, just as you once did. Don't label them anything but good because they tend to believe you and become what you say they are. Believe that they are good. Expect them to be good—not perfect. Encourage and appreciate the behavior you want.

Comparison

"There were four girls in our family," Laura told me. "We were always compared to each other in looks, intelligence, athletic ability, and so on. For the most part, I tried to 'hold my own' by competing with my sisters. My youngest sister felt defeated and reacted by not participating at all. Most of my self-esteem problems stem from the fact that I was never as 'wonderful' as my oldest sister." Comparison is a setup for low self-esteem. Did your parents compare you with your siblings? Did they play favorites? How did you feel when they did that? What were they trying to do? Did it work? What is your present relationship with your siblings: are you still competing?

Comparison makes our self esteem dependent on competition, which is a win-lose game. My success depends on your failure, and you are hoping that I will fail. Competition in every day family life leads to anxiety and loss of self-confidence, and damaged trust. Comparison interferes with cooperation and teamwork. No one really wins.

Competitiveness has been considered a national virtue that brings out the best in us. Perhaps this is true—on the sports field. Yet in more personal arenas, competition may make people suspicious and hostile toward others. Competition in schools prompts children to stop trying in order to prevent failure. Competitors are less apt to trust or communicate with one another; they see themselves as separate from one another, with conflicting goals. When I compete and compare myself with others, I can always feel like a failure because there's someone better than me in one area or another: she's got a better figure, he has a way with words, she makes more money.... All these thoughts can make me forget my own special gifts and qualities.

Often we trap ourselves by identifying the best qualities of many different people, synthesizing them into a fantasy ideal, and then try—as a single human being—to live up to that impossible image. We put others on a pedestal while putting ourselves down, and our self-esteem suffers in the process. If we put ourselves up and others down, we still drive wedges between us and create separation.

Comparison is a no-win situation. There are always people better or worse off than you. You feel smug or you feel guilty; either way gets you no where. Comparing yourself with others is not an accurate measure of your inherent self-worth.

With comparison, we separate ourselves from people by trying to be better than them—rather than enhancing our relationships by accepting our differences. Likewise, when we base our own judgment and behavior on someone else's values, we separate ourselves from our own truths. My daughter describes this phenomenon as "compara-sin"; it's a sin to give away so much of our power.

We can let go of the tendency to compete with everyone. We can let go of the win-lose struggle. We can learn instead to appreciate differences and to be sincerely happy for others' achievements and successes. As one woman stated, "Edna's a good cook, so let her cook. I'm a good eater!" This shift from win-lose to win-win thinking makes life less stressful and more fun. The win-win belief fosters cooperation which is essential for having a winning family team.

Cooperation is necessary for healthy families and also for success in business. A certain computer corporation began as a garage operation characterized by intense teamwork; now they seem to be taking over the world. Working and pulling together is the solid foundation on which successful businesses and winning families alike are built.

Comparison encourages and enforces conformity. But you don't have to be like everyone else! As a matter of fact, you *can't* be like everyone else, because you are one of a kind. It's okay to be who you really are. If you aren't you, who will be? Since the beginning of time, billions of people have inhabited our planet. Yet there has never been anyone like you. You are unique. You are special. Your personality plus your experiences make you a divine original. The only person you can really compare yourself with is you.

How are you today as compared with three months ago or three years ago? Are you more loving, more accepting? Are you a better person, or are you backsliding? Compare yourself only with you and your own personal growth. Compete only with yourself. Challenge yourself to become your own personal best.

Finally, when you notice that you are comparing yourself to (and competing with) another, change your self-talk. Instead of putting yourself down, consider the other person a model and lift yourself up. Even our children can be models. At my daughter's Junior High School I once observed her on stage moderating a program; I told myself that if she could do it, so could I! (Voila! Now, mysteriously, I am a professional speaker!) We are hungry for models. Seeing with new eyes, we can find people everywhere who can inspire us to excellence. When we can change our thinking from "you or me" to "you and me," we can enjoy ourselves and each other far more. We can feel a connection with, rather than a separation from others.

Seeing People as Objects

There are two ways of viewing people. In an I-Thou relationship, we can accept people as themselves and see them as they really are, but in an I-It relationship, we objectify them. Objectification of others—that is, seeing people as objects—has a natural use and value, as it helps us to organize the world. But it also forms the roots for racism and sexism, and personal alienation in our families and in society.

Seeing the world in terms of external or surface characteristics, e.g. nationality, race, sex, roles, handicaps, helps children simplify and organize a complex world. But the categories—the stereotypes—become filled with hand-me-down beliefs, fears, and other emotional baggage which can create distance, distrust, and disrespect. When people look for differences, that's all they see.

When I was young, my German family was the target of suspicion and prejudice during WWII. My uncle Franz, a quiet barber who spoke imperfect English, was suspected of being a Nazi. Hitler's army was the most horrifying expression of racism we have ever known, so the fear was understandable. Yet being associated with that stereotype was a threat to the entire family and frightened us all. Similarly, in California, thousands of Japanese Americans were rounded up and placed in concentration camps. Those victims of prejudice and fear suffered because they were seen as objects.

Growing up, we have all learned our own stereotypes: that it is not okay to be red or black, brown, yellow, Jewish, handicapped, gay, or female. Prejudice is generally taught subtly, but on a societal level, it is evident in unemployment, discrimination in education and higher level jobs, and low social status. The results are victimization, poverty, and low self-esteem in entire groups of people. If we internalize prejudice and social rejection, we can turn on ourselves and others like us.

Millions of people who fall into "minority" categories are ignored or treated like objects. They are not taken seriously. Negative judgements are based on a comparison of people in those groups to an "ideal" image of how they are supposed to be—according to stereotyped roles. These images often lie outside of our awareness until they are challenged in some way and brought to our consciousness.

There are also many gender stereotypes in our culture that interfere with communication. Macho men and seductive women are two of the most obvious; if couples play these games with one another, though, they will never learn to trust one another. This is why pornography is so dangerous. It reinforces the images that tell us that sex is loveless, women and children like to be hurt, and that treating people as objects is acceptable and normal. These things are not true, and they are far from normal. As a matter of fact, molesters of over 87% of girls and 77% of boys admitted to imitating behavior in pornographic publications. The porn industry sets up women—and young children—as objects of "pleasure" to be used and abused, and frighteningly enough, the largest consumers of pornography are impressionable children from 12 to 17 years of age.

Objectification dehumanizes people by stripping them of their individuality, their *person*-ality, and justifies treating them worse than machines. Its easy to be violent towards objects since objects don't have feelings.

We live in a culturally diverse society, where all people are created equal. Instead of putting ourselves and others down, we need to lift ourselves and others up. Instead of identifying with the lowest common denominators, we need to see the specialness in every human being. No matter what your race, ethnic origin, sex, or sexual preference, you are OKAY! You are a subject, not an object; you are you. To counter and heal destructive prejudice, affirm your own worth and that of others, e.g. black is beautiful—and white, yellow, and red are too. We have to rid ourselves of our mental shackles and join with our brothers and sisters for support, for healing, and for strengthening our pluralistic society.

Seeing Ourselves as Objects

If I have a picture in my head of how the "ideal you" is supposed to behave in an "ideal relationship," this means that an "ideal me" plays a certain role as well. When we expect ourselves to fit such images, the roles we play cut us off from any other reality—like who we really are. We acknowledge behavior that is consistent with our image, and filter out any information that doesn't fit. Therefore, we can share only certain parts of ourselves with others—and with ourselves. Controlling the world to fit my illusions, I can never honestly get to know myself—or you. I won't be able to accept you if you grow out of my ideal of you.

Objectifying ourselves leads to performance ("Smile for the camera!"), second-guessing, pretense, stress, and a lopsided focus on externals. We can spend a lifetime doing what we imagine others want us to do—only to find out that they never really wanted us to do that. A friend of mine and her husband moved to a new state. There, unsatisfied with their new house and location, they discovered that neither of them had actually wanted to move—but did it because each thought the other did! We can waste our lives never doing what we want, or even knowing what we want, because we're caught up in an imaginary structure that has little to do with reality.

Our images cause us a lot of trouble. Marriages hit the rocks when she realizes that "Mr. Right" can't be three places at once, or when the "perfect wife" suddenly loses her enthusiasm for keeping the "dream house" clean. How do healthy young parents respond when the apple of their eye is diagnosed with muscular dystrophy—or becomes handicapped in another way? What do upstanding, respectable parents do when their track star son announces he's gay? or when "daddy's little girl" becomes pregnant as a teenager? What happens when the image is shattered? What do we do when it's not happening the way it's "supposed to?"

Such crises force us to make a choice: between the image we have in our heads, and the real person in our lives, who is changing and growing—and who challenges us also to grow. Here's where we must face the alternative to "I-It" objectification, according to theologian Martin Buber, and create an "I-Thou" relationship. This shift challenges us to let go of rigid expectations and stereotypes that are too high, too low, or in conflict with the individual. The shift calls us to look deeper into the other person, seeing his or her capability rather than disability, looking beyond the differences to the commonality.

In the "I-Thou" approach, images and expectations of how people are supposed to be are put aside or suspended. We open our minds, instead, to see that person right now, without labels, without the distortion of past memories. We can see how they are changing. Instead of filtering out—denying—everything that doesn't fit our image, we are open and willing to let in new experiences and information. Instead of being judgmental, we can be compassionate.

This "I-Thou" relationship applies not only to our kids and spouses, but to friends and strangers, and, of course, to ourselves. Instead of going through the motions of playing your roles automatically, you can take a breath and make the shift to allow the inner process.

It's okay to be who you really are. If there are things you don't like about yourself, that's okay. In fact, it's important, as a parent, that you are first and foremost a real person. Then look at your kids, beyond the externals. See beyond their appearance, their performance, and their behaviors. See the beauty and richness that make them unique and lovable.

It's a relief to realize that you don't always have to be perfect for other people. You don't always have to be on top of things; you don't always have to be strong. You're human—with good and bad days. That's okay. When you accept your humanness (even the yucky parts), your kids will more readily accept theirs—and will show you their true, brilliant colors.

Making this shift brings excitement and aliveness; it presents a constantly changing and expanding world. It may also bring some discomfort as the old objectifying, dehumanizing ways thaw out and the "real world"—of emotions, insecurity, and exhilaration—rushes in. Communication is no longer guarded but is open to learning about oneself and others. This increases honesty and integrity, freedom, meaningful friendships, and personal growth.

It is important to be aware of our own thoughts and feelings. And it is equally important to be willing to let them go in order to be open to the exciting process of being human and to be able to understand, appreciate, and enjoy growth and change. Winning families are made up of people who constantly work to see themselves and others as dynamic, worthwhile persons, and not trap them as objects of the roles they play.

The Win-Lose System

The win-lose system, in which only one person wins and everyone else loses, is hard on self-esteem. Nobody likes to lose, yet mostly we're made to feel like losers. Often, focusing on faults and failures, people talk themselves into becoming losers.

We need to expand our definition of winning. Every success, accomplishment, achievement, every task crossed off a "to-do list" is a win! In the grocery store, putting milk into the cart is a win. We are winning all the time. Often, however, our wins go unnoticed and unappreciated by ourselves and others—and our self-esteem sags.

Pause for a moment and make a list of ten wins of the last few days. They can be big or little achievements—for example, getting to work or school on time, asking for something you wanted, changing seventeen diapers without complaining, or fixing a nice dinner for the family last night. Now give yourself a big pat on the back. You deserve it because you are a winner. You deserve more appreciation. Yet you can't appreciate something if you don't notice it. So start looking for the wins.

When you crawl into bed tonight, don't think of what you didn't finish, what you should have done, what you could have done better. Instead, look for the wins. Every night before you turn off the light, make a list of ten things you did well, and you'll sleep like a baby. The next day, you will wake up feeling refreshed and positive about your life.

Instead of hoping that someone will notice and appreciate you, *give that to yourself.* You know when you did a good job; tell yourself so. Give yourself a pat on the back. Appreciation for ourselves and others can turn duty into a gift. It makes us much healthier and more fun to be around. A "winning is everything" attitude in life and sports can devastate self-esteem.

Sports have a powerful, long-lasting impact on children's lives. Coaches, teachers, and parents—with good intentions—may cause humiliation and frustration, anger and anxiety, failure and rejection in kids which will last much longer than the season. Yet if the child is treated with dignity, encouragement, and support, being on the team can foster a sense of belonging, self-confidence, and fun. How the game is played and coached is as important as winning.

Positive self-esteem is essential for mental health and happiness. It is a necessary ingredient of a winning family. Yet our culture is very hard on self-esteem, presenting many barriers to mental health and happiness. We do our best based on the information we have. Yet frequently our knowledge is incomplete, or we are misinformed, or believe in myths that do not apply to our lives. When what we know is incorrect, things don't work out. "I did everything I was supposed to" I once exclaimed. "Why do I feel so bad?"

Now that you are aware of some of the barriers, they will become merely stumbling blocks. You can seek out solid information, unlearn what doesn't work and learn what does. Then you can pass on better information to your kids so they can have their feet on solid ground sooner than you did. Once we see clearly, we can help our children avoid the pitfalls in their own lives. Once we identify the stumbling blocks, we can turn them into stepping stones for personal growth and higher self-esteem.

Questions

The questions
Which frighten and make us want to run,
Which evade our socialized minds,
Which have never before been asked—
These are the questions which
We must dare to pursue,
The edges we must explore.

—L. Hart[5]

21.

Who's Pulling Your Strings?

"To be nobody but yourself in a world which is doing its best to make you just like everybody else means to fight the greatest battle there is or ever will be."

—e.e. cummings[1]

For most of my life I did just what I was "supposed" to do. On a day-to-day basis, I automatically carried out the inner musts, have tos, and ought tos that had been running my life. Then I learned the twelfth commandment: "Thou shalt not should upon thyself".[2]

I started to listen to my self-talk one day soon after. Surprised at the string of orders bossing me around, I tuned in more closely. When I heard, "You have to wash the kitchen floor," I looked over my shoulder, wondering who'd said that. I sat myself down and had a little talk with myself. "Self," I asked, "do you *choose* to clean the kitchen floor?" "Well," my Self answered, "I can't walk barefoot anymore." After this little discussion, I decided that I *wanted* to wash the floor so I could walk barefoot and enjoy it. Doing this chore, then, wasn't half bad, because *I had chosen to do it!* That was the beginning of the long, gradual shift toward discovering my internal locus of control.

Growing up is the process of making the shift from an external to an internal authority, or locus of control. When children are little, they have an external locus of control. They look to their parents and other important adults for information, for values, for direction. Like little sponges, they absorb and accept everything in their environment—believing it—and they internalize it. As they develop and mature, they gradually learn to think for themselves, trust themselves, become themselves. They learn to stand on their own two feet. They gain in confidence and competence. Ideally, as parents empower them and let go of control, children assume more responsibility and control over their own lives.

For many people, however, this important developmental process has been interrupted or thwarted; many adults who were not empowered by their parents, still trust others more than they trust themselves. They are overly concerned about what *others* might say, what *others* might think, and what might please or displease others. (You *know* you're in big trouble if you're afraid to touch the pillow tags that say "Do not remove under penalty of law!") Many look to other people and things for approval or for a sense of worth or for happiness. Many still look to others to clean up after themselves or to rescue them from problems. Many have never discovered their own values, beliefs, habits, and identity.

External locus of control people tend to be extremely dependent on persons and things outside of themselves; they give their power away, then feel powerless and out of control. In neglecting their own values, desires, dreams, and intuition, they lack identity and individuality. These people are the ones who, if their physician tells them they have six months to live, they die obediently right on schedule. Seeking solutions outside of themselves, they are vulnerable to manipulation and exploitation by others and can easily become addicted to unhealthy relationships, drugs, food, entertainment, work, and possessions.

Unfortunately, our western consumer culture is much too concerned with external things. Our appearance, performance, achievements, and possessions are given tremendous importance. (Americans have four hundred times more possessions now than in the 1940s!) The internal—what *we* think, what *we* need, what *we* value, what gives *us* meaning in life—is often ignored or considered unimportant. Thus, we are encouraged to remain children—dependent on external displays of identity, external sources of self-worth. We yield our power to vague external authorities of fashion, fads, and status symbols.

Yet, if we look around, we notice that the most interesting, impressive, and expressive people we know are the ones who have, at some point, decided to take charge of their lives. The truly successful people are the ones who succeed *in their own terms*—by writing their own rules and becoming their own authority. Dr. Bernie Siegel, author of *Love, Medicine, and Miracles,* writes about his exceptional cancer patients—the ones who are exceptions to the rule that cancer is incurable:

> Exceptional patients manifest the will to live in its most potent form. They take charge of their lives even if they were never able to before, and they work hard to achieve health and peace of mind. They do not rely on doctors to take the initiative but rather use them as members of a team, demanding the utmost in technique, resourcefulness, concern, and openmindedness. If they're not satisfied, they change doctors.[3]

These people have found their inner locus of control and their lives will never be the same again because they have found their inner wisdom. Yet we do not have to go to the threshold of death to find it. We can give ourselves permission now.

Well, where is *your* locus of control? Do you do things more to please others or to please yourself? Do you listen more to the external voices—the musts, have tos, ought tos—or do you listen more to your secret internal voices—your intuition.

Begin today to find your inner locus of control: make a list of five things that you have to, ought to, or are supposed to do today. Start each sentence with "I". Then rewrite your list, beginning each sentence, instead, with "I choose to." Notice the difference you feel.

Now *you* are in control. As an adult, you have power over your own life. You have created the life you now live and can make changes.

Turn off the television, the radio, and the walkman. Relax! Then listen. Turn down the endless bombardment of noise and chatter. Listen! Listen to the soft inner voice. Then do what is good for you. Quiet time can be the most important time in your life. Take long walks. Listen to your body. Learn to trust it. Meditate. Write in a journal. These are the ways you can practice "inner listening"—the guidance system that "makes clearer to us what we really want, as distinct from what we have been talked into."[4] Learn to trust your self. Use your own mind and body, and you're an autonomous adult—your own person.

In raising a family, we begin with externally oriented little children who learn their value (and everything else) from the important people in their lives. Parents can nudge them toward becoming internally oriented adults who can think for themselves, who can trust themselves, and who have internalized self-esteem and personal power.

Here are suggestions to nurture the internal development of your children:

- Develop and enjoy the bond of love between you and your kids.
- Accept them *as they are* (though not necessarily all their behaviors). Give them permission to be individuals. Provide understanding, support, and nurturing.
- Accept and understand their needs and feelings. Your children are unique beings with their own ideas and desires.
- Honor their separateness from you. When possible, let them do things their own way. Give them permission to be individuals. Let *them* teach *you.*
- Encourage them to think for themselves, to make decisions and goals based on what *they* want and need, what *they* think is best.

147

If "everybody's doing it", assist your kids in sorting out the situation and consequences, and help them decide what *they* feel is right.

- Offer choices. (Would you rather have your birthday party at home or in the park this year?)
- Listen to their experiences, stories, and opinions.
- Support and encourage healthy exploration of their world while setting reasonable and healthy limits.
- Use assertive communication instead of games, force, and manipulation.
- Use the natural and logical consequences style of discipline. It teaches children to figure things out, to think for themselves, and to become self- disciplined.
- Use more encouragement and less praise. Praise is a verbal reward that shows children that they are pleasing to others. Encouragement motivates them *from within*—from being pleased with themselves. The child observes the support, knows that you believe in him or her, achieves something, and gains higher self-esteem *directly* from the experience.
- Give your child a box of stars. Let them be in charge of rewarding themselves.
- Encourage your kids to take quiet time in the afternoon. They may complain of boredom at first. That's okay. A classmate once pointed out that the most creative and best times of her childhood came shortly after she announced that she was bored. Instead of looking for external satisfaction, she looked within and discovered exciting internal resources.

You can foster this growth in your children as you cultivate it in yourself. As you get in touch with your own inner wisdom, you can trust that it will guide you in the fine art of parenting. You can become one family of centered individuals, leading your own interesting and healthy lives.

"My advice", writes, surgeon Bernie Siegel, "is to live *your* life.... The blueprint for you to be your authentic self lies within.... In some mystical way, the microscopic egg that grew to be you had the program for your physical, intellectual, emotional, and spiritual development. Allow the development to occur to its fullest; grow and bloom. Follow your bliss and be what you want to be."[5]

22.

Play

"One joy scatters a hundred griefs."

—Chinese Proverb

I once attended a kazoo concert—a "Kazoophony." The musicians (who claimed to have attended the Eastman Kazoovatory of Music) played "The 1813 Overture," and "The Plight of the Kazoomblebee." The kazoo, they said, is to classical music what a total body cast is to ballet. Needless to say, it was not an evening of soaring and inspiring elegance, but those performers sure rediscovered silliness—and they are rewarded for it, by bringing joy and laughter into people's lives.

Play is a universal language and one of the healthiest things in our culture. When we play, we give a gift of joy & spontaneity to one another. The thrill of being alive pervades our entire body when we play. Families—and life—are supposed to be fun.

"Take me into your world," I once told my children, "and show me what you see." Leaving my parent-self at home, we walked along the irrigation ditch to the bridge where the troll lives. We stopped along the narrow path in front of a crooked tree ("Put your feet right here, Mom, stoop down, and squint") they showed me where to look to see the Dr. Seuss creature in the trunk. I had passed that way many times before, but I had never been able to see it before! This was my initiation into their magical, mystical and wonder-full world. That experience bridged the worlds of parent and child in which we each lived, separately, and that memory enriches me still.

Children are our natural teachers, but to learn best from them, we must meet them at their level. They can help us remember how to play—how to break all the rules and write our own. A chair can be a fort or a fire engine; an adult can be the baby when the kids play "house." My children have encouraged me to try new games—like hackey-sack or riding a skateboard—and have helped me to remember some wonderful old ones like Hide and Seek and squirt-gun fights. Through our children, we can see the world with fresh eyes. With them we can cut loose from stuffy adultness, be totally foolish—and get away with being unforgivably silly! We can reclaim forgotten parts of ourselves and rediscover the finer points of childhood.

What did you love to do as a kid? Remember those adventures and tricky games? Share them with your kids! Have you shared your jacks and marbles with them? If kids don't learn to play when they are young, they may never learn.

To many kids with a high TV diet, play means passively waiting to be entertained; they don't learn to actively entertain themselves. Putdowns, humiliation, and violence are often the forms of "humor" we find on television; canned laughter marks the pauses where the watching audience is "supposed to" laugh. Kids learn from commercials that they can't play without the expensive games and toys that are in fashion at the time. They need encouragement to discover their own creativity through the excitement of building a dam or a treehouse from scratch.

My older kids are among the first generation that has grown up with television. My daughter, in her late teens, once complained that to most people her age fun meant watching TV movies and/or drinking beer. If the drinks are half price, it's Happy Hour; if there's no free beer at a party, it's reason enough not to go. So they sit around building addictions and wondering, "Are we having fun yet?"

Kids are born with inner joy. Play is as natural to them as breathing. For kids, there is no separation between work and play. Work is play until parents teach them that it's work—only then do they learn to resist it. They quickly pick up the dualistic thinking of the adult world: work is what you have to do and don't like, and play is what you love to do but don't have time for. Yet work can become play with an adult's attitude shift. Having a vegetable garden, for example, can be drudgery for you as a parent, or it can be a joy. If we put fun back into our own work, we will *want* to do it and our kids will be more eager to join in.

Childhood is a time of phenomenal growth, aliveness, and discovery. Growing up, for many, has meant ending this amazing process. A young man once said to me, "Growing up in America is the process of growing numb." Many have come to associate growing up with a loss of excitement and eagerness to learn. Playfulness has slowly disappeared from their lives. Yet this need not be a terminal condition. Ask a kid how to play, and you can recapture dormant parts of yourself, bringing aliveness, spontaneity, and joy back into your life.

When my kids were young, I collected rhythm instruments. Periodically we would turn on some lively music, and all become percussionists. Sometimes we took out hats—or made them—to add to the fun and marched and paraded around the house. (My husband and I sometimes took the rhythm toys out for adult parties, giving the cymbals to the most reserved person there.) (Note: this always worked.)

We also acted out "Peter and the Wolf." I'd put on the record, and the living room was suddenly transformed into a meadow, each of us playing a character and identifying with the instruments and themes. There was almost always an argument over who got to be who, but this charade was a wonderful way to spend an evening together. Strangely enough, my kids as adults all still like to express themselves to classical music....

If you aren't already playing with your kids, here are some tips:

- Play needs to be fun for everyone. When you tease or tickle your kids, watch them; if it's not fun for them, stop doing it. Some parents toss a baby into the air, saying "What fun!" and continue even if the baby starts to cry. If you're both not having fun, change the game. Kids may feel violated by well-meaning parents and older siblings who tease them too far.

- Play is best when everyone comes out winning. If you really want your kids to win, you will coach and cheer for them and be happy when they succeed. "New Games" are non-competitive games that involve everyone. Tail of the Dragon, for example, involves a line of people, each holding on to the waist of the person in front of them. A kerchief (the tail) hangs from the pocket of the last person, and the first person (the head) trys to catch it.

- When parents "have to" beat their kids at a game, the kids are set up to lose. This isn't play, but a power ploy with the losers being victimized. Parents are bigger, older, and smarter than kids; they can win all the time if they want. Yet kids who lose all the time become discouraged and don't want to play anymore because they know they will lose. Nobody likes to lose. The parent may win the game, but the relationship suffers as does the child's attitude toward play. If your parents played with you in this way, remember how it felt. Did you ever shrug and say, "It doesn't matter" when it did? That kind of play wasn't fair—and it wasn't fun. Try a new kind of game with your kids, or let them win sometimes.

- There's folk wisdom that states, "A dirty kid is a happy kid." To tell your kid, "Go out and play but don't get dirty" is a setup for disappointment. Kids often do get dirty when they're having a good time. A dirty, excited kid may be healthier than a clean, but depressed one.

Playing will develop your sense of humor—and that of your kids. A regular dose of giggles and snorts does wonderful—even astonishing things for your emotional and physical health and well-being.

Norman Cousins was told by his physicians that he had a chronic, debilitating disease. He refused to believe that he would only get worse, then die. He decided to do anything necessary to defeat the disease process. If we can create disease in our bodies by negative thoughts, beliefs, and attitudes, he reasoned, we also have the power to reverse that process and create healthy bodies instead.

Every day Cousins watched old Charlie Chaplin movies and laughed until his sides ached. He filled his hospital room with laughter and giggles. Over time he succeeded in reversing his "terminal" disease, and regained perfect health![1] So laugh often—there's always something to laugh at—it will make you healthy.

Not only does laughter stimulate the immune system, it relaxes you and raises your guard against depression and pain. Exercise is a form of play for many—running, dancing, hiking, swimming, and biking—and the people you play and laugh with easily become your friends. Play in a family increases health, happines, and harmony. It creates bonds between people and enhances personal growth and self-esteem. A gift that keeps giving, your play of today builds a store of rich memories for you to draw upon as time moves along.

For those who don't enjoy themselves, life is a burden, others can be a burden, and they are a burden to themselves. Enjoying yourself, on the other hand, is one of the greatest things you can do for yourself. And because joy is contagious, others will also benefit.

Kids are a great excuse to be silly. Alone, you might not spontaneously roll down a grassy hill, lest someone think you berserk, but if you take a kid along, no one will think twice. If they do, it will probably be, "How wonderful to see parents playing with their children!"

Seek out and share natural highs with your family—adventures, art, making music, cuddling, laughter, excitement. Look for beautiful sunsets and rainbows. Share the amazement, the awe with each other. Be silly at times; silly is not a four letter word. It's good to be silly and to allow that in your kids. It's a sign of aliveness; depressed children are not silly. Natural highs may be an important key to alcohol and drug abuse prevention. When people are high on life, they don't need alcohol and drugs.

One of our peak experiences happened as my kids and I were at the edge of a small lake catching pollywogs. My youngest proudly brought a giant tadpole to show me, opened his hand, and discovered that he could feel its heart beating! He gave it to me so I could feel the pulse. The magic and mystery of that moment still thrill me.

Start to play today. Look for things that tickle your funny bone. Put down this book and do one fun thing you love to do. Right now. It's never too late to have a happy childhood; you deserve joy in your life! Make fun time a high priority in your family. Set aside a half day to play together. Go for a walk or a bikeride. Go to museum or to the zoo. Also, be silly with your kids *at least* once a day.

Family playtime increases closeness and positive feelings. Everyone relaxes and feels more alive. Love just happens when you're having fun together. Tape this one on your refrigerator: *The Family That Plays Together, Stays Together!*

23.

The Winning Environment

*"If a seed is given good soil and plenty of water and sun,
it doesn't have to try to unfold.
It doesn't need self-confidence or self-discipline or perseverance.
It just unfolds. As a matter of fact, it can't help unfolding."*

—Barbara Sher[1]

Human beings need optimal growing conditions in order to thrive. For those who did not have them as a child, growth and development may have been impaired. Yet seeds may lie dormant for a long time until the environment improves—the sun shines, the rain comes, a rock is moved away. Then they can grow, blossom, and bear fruit.

Remembering your family environment as a child, consider the following questions.

- Could you trust your parents—knowing that they would take care of your needs (food, shelter, acceptance, and love) and protect you from harm?
- Were you respected and loved just for being you?
- Did your parents realize that you were unique and special and make you feel that way?
- Did they believe in you and encourage you to be your best?
- Did you feel that your ideas and opinions were taken seriously?
- Were you encouraged to discover and explore your special talents and interests?
- Did they encourage you to do things for yourself—including solving your own problems?
- Did they both set limits and allow freedom?
- Were you told that you could be and do anything you wanted? Were you given support and encouragement to do so?
- Did you know that when you got in over your head you could turn to them for help—without reproach?[2]

If you answered yes to many of these questions, yours was probably a winning environment. If you answered with many no's, you must realize that you've had some obstacles to high self-esteem—but your parents probably gave you more than they had received. They probably did the best they could at parenting, which is the most difficult and challenging job of all. Your parents made mistakes, as we all do; learn from them and forgive them. Be grateful for all the good things they gave you.

We are all winners. Yet, some people are disguised as losers. In their childhood environment, perhaps no one saw their beauty or made them feel beautiful. Perhaps no one saw their hidden greatness and the important gifts they had for the world. Perhaps no one believed in them, supported them, or encouraged them to become winners. They became losers because they had no idea that they really were winners.

Many people who lacked important emotional nutrients as children become late bloomers. They fill their areas of deficiency, and learn new skills. They grow, blossom, and bear fruit. It's never too late to become the beautiful, healthy, and happy person you were meant to be.

Imagine how different your life would be now if you had grown up in a winning environment. Imagine what your family of today might become if you were to create a winning environment. All children have the potential for becoming winners. If they can be winners in their own families, they are on the road to a successful life.

It all begins with a decision. You can use all the tools in this book—affirming yourself and your children, finding new ways to talk and play together.... You can make big changes a little at a time. You cannot turn back the clock. But you can begin now.

As you create a healthier environment for your children, you create it for yourself; as you create it for yourself, you create it for your children. At first it may be hard work—change is usually difficult. But it will get easier and better. Be patient. It takes time. Each little change is a movement toward becoming a Winning Family.

24.

Extending
Your Family

*"The bond that links your true family is not one of blood,
but of respect and joy in each other's life."*

—Richard Bach[1]

Before 1936, most American families were multigenerational extended families. They were not only the center of work, education, recreation, and worship; they also constituted economic production units. In rural settings, cooperation was necessary for survival.

Kids would see how grandparents, aunts, and uncles got along with others, how they made judgments and decisions, how they solved problems. They would get outside opinions from various people they trusted. They watched adults handle important human emotions and major life events: marriage, childbirth, sickness, and death. If a parent died, aunts and uncles could fill in to keep the family going.

Rubbing elbows with lots of relatives, children learned to get along with different types of people. Many adults shared responsibility for the children. Working side by side with others, children got direct on-the-job training for living.

I grew up in an extended family in Detroit. My German-immigrant parents met there and married shortly after. My father's brother, Franz, lived with the family for twenty years. Uncle Franz was a barber. As a child, I would sit on his lap and comb his hair. I would walk with him to visit his friends. I saw his world and how he related to it. I learned much from him. Sharing special time together, we developed a loving bond between us. His presence in my family was a key to my self-esteem.

Families have changed dramatically—from the extended family, to the nuclear family, and now to an amazing diversity of family forms. Children of today grow up in a variety of family units. One in five children lives in a "blended" or stepfamily. One in four lives in a single-parent family. More than half the children under age six are cared for by a childcare provider while parents work. And there are 2 million "latchkey children" who must be responsible for themselves during afterschool hours.

Today we have smaller households; a greater proportion have few or no children, and there are an increasing number of single-person households—families of one. Individuals are more isolated, more alone. A man I know commented that when he was growing up, neighbors would always poke their heads through the kitchen door in the morning and ask, "Is the coffee on?" Where he lives today, he is on speaking terms with the neighbors, but only to the point of making small talk about the car or the weather. The days of neighborhoods serving as community support groups are all but gone.

Every year in the United States, 40 million people move from one place to another.[2] They uproot themselves for a variety of reasons; many move great distances, leaving grandparents, friends and neighbors behind. Some move to withdraw from the pain and problems of dysfunctional families. Some move to pursue job or educational opportunities. Transplanting their families to new settings, they must start over from the beginning—re-creating important connections with others.

Within the last fifty years there have been enormous splits in families—physically and emotionally; the two often go hand in hand. For many, important natural family connections have been seriously weakened or severed.

In the case of divorce, for example, the vital grandparent-grandchild bond is frequently interrupted or damaged at a time when kids most desperately need support and stability. In the past, aunts and uncles and grandparents often filled in during times of crisis until the family recovered. Kids had someone familiar to cling to throughout the turmoil.

Divorce stems from problems between husband and wife. It need not create a major rift between two families. The kids are not divorcing a parent, nor grandparents, aunts, or uncles. They should not lose those special people at a time when they most need loving support. Non-custodial parents can have a tremendous influence in the life and self-esteem of their children. It's important to maintain a strong, loving bond. Give them time (high quality visits), attention (letters and phone calls), and pay attention to their needs. The human connections are more important than the roles you play in a family system.

It is possible for divorced couples to heal their wounds over time and even become friends with each other. In this new style of extended family, there is less pain and harm to the kids and the rest of the family. I have a friend who is on such good terms with her ex-husband (and his second wife) that she is godmother to their two children, and although they live over a thousand miles apart, they see each other at least once a year.

Mothers-in-law have inherited an unfortunate cultural stereotype. Unfairly labeled "the enemy," they are the butt of many jokes that set them up for rejection, divisiveness, and pain. The same is true for stepmothers. Although it is difficult to blend two families, negative stereotypes can undermine the quality of the grandparent-grandchild, stepparent-stepchild connection.

Grandparents are natural self-esteem developers, yet they often live too far away to maintain close contact with their children. These greatest of natural resources for making kids feel important may themselves be feeling unimportant, lonely, and unneeded hundreds of miles away. This loving cross-generational kinship connection has been dangerously weakened. Yet it need not be this way.

Helen, a seventy-six year old grandmother in one of my workshops, works in a nursery school. After her own six children were grown, she got involved working with other people's kids. She loves doing it, and knows she's needed. And the children are enriched with her loving presence, her depth of experience, and her wisdom. Kids in nursery schools and daycare centers everywhere would benefit from involvement of loving grandparents.

Everyone needs someone to turn to when things are tough. The hard work of childrearing is lightened by having someone share laughter, a meal, a walk in the park. "Joy shared is joy doubled; sorrow shared is sorrow cut in half."

When my children were young, a sixteen-year-old boy from Mississippi lived with our nuclear family for a summer. Paul did yard work for us and at times helped with the kids. We all enjoyed our "extended family" so much that we invited him back the following year. Now, despite the miles that separate us, a loving bond connects us with him. Paul is part of our family.

Later on, my daughter extended the family even further. Attending college in Santa Fe, she interviewed with a family looking for a babysitter for their three young sons. It was love at first sight and gradually Kristen became part of their family just as Paul had become part of ours. Moving in with them, she continued a pattern she had learned was acceptable and desirable in her childhood. When we visited her for the holidays, we were graciously, lovingly and openly taken in by her adopted family.

New varieties of extended families are becoming more widespread today. Consciously or unconsciously, people are seeking out others to fill the void created by the absence of family members. Co-workers may become siblings or cousins. Neighbors may fill in as aunts, uncles, or grandparents. Many families are sharing their kids, spreading the responsibility around a bit, creating the support they need, and enriching their lives.

After creating a "surrogate family," Kathy (a workshop participant) reflected, "Our biological families contain structured roles that lock us into a track of behavior much like a roller-coaster. As we grow and change, it becomes difficult to break away from these predefined roles. The surrogate family, by contrast, begins at the point at which we left the biological one. There are few preconceived notions about us, and we're allowed to be ourselves. We can interact without the fear of criticism or comparison. We can *choose* our surrogate family members."

Many couples, with or without children, are choosing to have another person share their homes with them. The honesty and realness that happen in live-in situations can create deep bonds. There is, of course, increased possibility for friction, but there is also increased opportunity for enrichment. These roommates become part of each other's lives—even after they have separated.

In 1936 a group of twelve young mothers from a farm community in Colorado formed a social club called The Diligent Dozen so that they could go somewhere with their children and completely enjoy themselves. They had all moved west with their husbands and met monthly with each other to do mending and fancy work while their children played. Afterward they enjoyed games that had been planned by the hostess. The husbands, who affectionately called the club The Dirty Dozen, were welcome if they came. They had big feasts at holidays. As original members passed away over the years, they invited new women to join. Through repeated contact, they developed a deep bond—"like family"—among themselves.[3]

People who have on-going significant contact with children—childcare providers, babysitters, neighbors—are part of their extended family. They play very important roles in children's lives, in their development. As kids get older, they may seek out and "adopt" surrogate family members who can enrich their lives as well as our own.

The Mexican-American culture actively adds new members to "la familia". The best man and maid of honor at weddings and sponsors in baptism and confirmation ceremonies become "padrinos" and a part of the family. These multi-generational families keep expanding their connections.

We need many caring people in our lives. We need to come together in ways that matter, that sustain and enrich us. We can share ourselves and our children. When we extend our families, we expand our lives.

25.

The Winning Family

"The greatest gifts you can give your children are the roots of responsibility and the wings of independence."

—Denis Waitly[1]

Winning families come in a variety of forms, sizes, and colors. They have qualities in common that contribute to a high level of self-worth in their members. The climate is comfortable; people feel "at home" in their homes.

There is a strong sense of sharing and connectedness in a family team. Members know that they are important, that they belong. Yet given the wings of independence, they are encouraged to find and create their own meaning and purpose in life and to realize their own dreams. Balancing closeness and separateness, they enjoy spending time together, and apart. Individuals do their own thing and are also committed to the well-being of others, of the whole family.

One spring, my sons created a memorable winning event. Damian (age 23) offered to be the chauffeur for Felix's senior prom. He borrowed a Mercedes-Benz from a professor, decorated the inside with silk roses, and dressed for the part. Being short on money, Felix and his friend Jeff decided to cook dinner at our home. I ironed my best tablecloth and borrowed a silver candelabra and serving pieces.

The boys spent many hours shopping and cooking. Suddenly it was time to put on their tuxedos and leave. Damian chauffeured Felix to pick up his date while I picked up the pieces in the kitchen. Later, exchanging cap for apron, the chauffeur became the waiter. He served the lobster tails which he presented as "giant roly-polys".[2] Felix snapped his fingers nonchalantly and called for the (nonalcoholic) wine. With a flourish, Damian opened the wired-on champagne cap and uncovered a screw-on cap, which everyone sniffed without cracking a smile. In the kitchen, I was loving every minute of it!

The winning family operates on the principle that *everyone* has a right to come out "on top." This team encourages and supports all its players in discovering their unique interests and talents. Through believing in, coaching, and helping one another, they set themselves up for success. No one has to lose.

Parents become a winning example—in an area of importance to them—and they let their own lives show the way. They want to be successful and set themselves up to do so; they model winning. They also want their spouses and kids to win and set them up to do so, too. "If I help you meet your goals, I win; if you help me reach mine, you win." That everyone can come out winning is an underlying belief. No one, therefore, has a desire to win at another's expense.

To create a Winning Family, it is necessary to redefine winning. Winning can no longer be defined as competing with, overpowering, intimidating, and putting others down. That is the win-lose model. A new definition of winning is to be your best and do the best you can. A desire for excellence—in oneself and for others—is the trait of a real winner.

Winning Families are made up of high quality relationships based on mutual respect, acceptance, honesty, trust, cooperation, loyalty, and faith in others. The parents honestly know and accept themselves, including their feelings and weaknesses. They can, therefore, accept feelings and weaknesses in each other and in their children. The win-win belief is relational; one can't be a winner without caring, sharing, and empowering others to win.

The well-being of individuals is a very high priority. Rules—as few as possible and as many as necessary—are made for the benefit of the whole family, not just the rulemaker. Rules validate and promote self-worth in individuals and harmony in the family. Parents create rules that say that human life and feelings are more important than anything else.

In winning families, people are listened to and heard. They enjoy spending time with each other. Everything is out in the open; there is no need for secrets or dishonesty. Family members are genuine with each other; they don't have to pretend or play a role. They know they are accepted and loved for who they are.

This healthy family has an openness to new people and new ideas. The whole family system is adaptable to life's changes—including new role definitions—and accepts and encourages change as a potential source of growth.

The climate is characterized by aliveness, genuineness, and love. It is okay to take risks. It is safe to be honest and real. A winning family is a high self-esteem team.

The "Perfect Family" model that is held up to us as an ideal never has problems. Everyone is always happy, always smiling, always clean. Expectations of perfection—to be a perfect parent, a perfect husband or wife, or a perfect kid—are setups for frustration, disappointment, anger, pretense, and low self-esteem. The perfect family is a myth. It is a performance—like posing for a snapshot—that is a barrier to intimacy. It creates a great deal of stress when confused with real life.

On the other hand, the Winning Family is like a moving picture in which things are always happening, where people are changing and growing. A winning family is always in process. Of course they have problems—everyone has problems—but they have skills to deal with them and the confidence that they will overcome them. When they need help, they have the wisdom to get it.

You can create a Winning Family—a family in which everyone feels like a success. It's very difficult to do in our win-lose culture. But it's worth the effort. There's great joy and a depth of connection that can happen when you replace old negative habits with new high self-esteem behavior and attitudes. It all begins with a decision.

The Winning Family has nothing to do with awards or trophies. It has to do with liking, loving, and enjoying each other. It has to do with satisfaction. A Winning Family feels good.

A Winning Family begins with parents who have a high level of self-worth—the higher their own self-esteem and sense of competence, the more likely they are to create a Winning Family team. It begins with the desire for everyone to be a success within the family and with a decision to learn and apply the skills to make that happen.

Postscript: On Nightmares

"Until now, every generation throughout history lived with the tacit certainty that other generations would follow. Each assumed, without questioning, that its children and children's children and those yet unborn would carry on—to walk the same earth, under the same sky."

—Joanna Rogers Macy[1]

As parents, we give our children the gift of life—and the necessary tools to live it well. We need to protect them from harm and give them comfort during nightmares, assuring them that all will be okay. Yet our children are growing up in a nightmare. We are all living in a nightmare. And we don't know how it will turn out.

Children are aware of the danger of global annihilation. They know of the possibility of planetary extinction. Realizing that they may not have a chance to grow up—or that the earth may die under their feet—they can feel confused, angry, powerless, desperate.

Never since the beginning of time has there been such danger to ourselves, our children, and our grandchildren. Toxic wastes, acid rain, rising rates of radioactivity, dying lakes and seas, loss of topsoil and forestland, global warming, and expiring species of plants and animals are all signs of the progressive destruction of the very systems that support our existence. The air we breathe, the food and water we give our children, are often polluted. These are life-threatening realities. In the last 25 years, serious birth defects have doubled around the world.[2]

We must protect our children. In the words of science-fiction writer Robert Heinlein, "A society that does not protect its young is doomed."

We are all dependent on the functioning of things beyond our control; economics, information systems, and energy resources are only partially in the hands of human beings. Things like the weather and gravity are not.

When the earth moves, as it did October 17 in the San Francisco

Bay Area, all these things are put into perspective. Within fifteen seconds of the shock, people knew what really mattered in this life. Phone lines jammed as millions around the world reached out to their family and friends. The first question: Is the family okay? The jolt brought people back to basics. One man commented, "We're alive and healthy; the rest is only money." The earthquake reconnected people to what they were based on—a spiritual connection with loved ones and an awareness of our mysterious connection with Mother Earth whom we can no longer take for granted.

We are profoundly interconnected with the earth: as the earth has changed, we have been changed. This works both ways. Over the years, more humans have acquired more things and become more wasteful. We have greatly abused and exploited our planet. And as humans have changed, the earth has been changed. Our environment is now in crisis and we must do all we can to heal the damage we've done.

Understanding our interconnectedness and the cause-effect relationships, it is obvious that we must stop our irresponsible and destructive ways. We must curtail our excessive consumption and become aware of our role in the destruction of the land or we will not survive as a people. We must learn to walk lightly on the earth and respect her as deeply as we do ourselves and each other. Let us learn to live in harmony with others and with the earth. Our deepest human bonds are grounded in our bond with Mother Earth.

"No other generation has inherited this enormous responsibility and the privilege of saving all past and all future generations, all animals and all plants," states Australian pediatrician Helen Caldicott.[3] Now is a hard time to be a kid—or a parent. Yet, it is also an exciting time. We are living on the edge of a breakthrough.

We need to look at our beliefs about the earth. If we say, "The problems we face are so immense; whatever I do wouldn't matter," we overwhelm ourselves. We talk ourselves into being helpless and hopeless.

If, instead, we tell ourselves that we must heal the planet for the sake of our children and grandchildren, we empower ourselves. We do something and something changes. I remember the first Earth Day back in the '60s; my young children filled several bags with the trash that had littered a picnic area. When they were a little older, we all marched on the capitol and stopped the Vietnam War. When parents care enough to get involved, it gives children a sense of purpose and hopefulness.

We need to look at our beliefs—about war and peace. If we believe that war is inevitable, we develop a victim mentality, saying to ourselves, "My life is at the mercy of forces beyond my control. There's nothing I can do." In thinking this way, we disempower ourselves. We do nothing. Nothing changes. We feel afraid and desperate.

If, on the other hand, we choose to believe that peace is possible—and that it is our responsibility—it's very different. We tell ourselves, "I can make a difference. I know I can. If it's to be, it's up to me." We look for opportunities to become involved. We join with others who share our concern. We empower ourselves and each other to take action. We feel hopeful. We act and things change. Even if our contributions are small, they make a big difference.

Bringing a child into the world is the greatest act of hope there is. It is our statement of trust that life will go on—that we will enjoy our children and our children's children. We must hope, but we can no longer take the future for granted. We gave birth to our children. Now we must give birth to a healthy world where they will thrive.

In understanding the qualities of winning families—respect, responsibility, caring, seeing cause and effect relationships, fixing mistakes and learning from them, believing that it's unethical to "win" while damaging others (and the earth)—we understand some principles for winning communities and for a winning world.

We must hold ourselves and our children accountable—and also our political leaders. Let us remind them that our American democracy was founded on a government of the people, by the people, and for the people—of present and future generations. As they discuss the priorities and values of the country (as reflected in the national budget), let us speak up for "all our relations" as the native peoples say—to improve the quality of life for families in America. Let us accept our responsibility and the challenge to make the world a truly safe and healthy environment for ourselves and our loved ones.

A healthy and peaceful world is the best setting for a Winning Family. And a Winning Family is the best foundation for a Winning World.

Appendix A

FIFTY YEARS FROM NOW
IT WILL NOT MATTER
WHAT KIND OF CAR YOU DROVE,
WHAT KIND OF HOUSE YOU LIVED IN,
HOW MUCH YOU HAD IN YOUR BANK ACCOUNT,
NOR WHAT YOUR CLOTHES LOOKED LIKE.
BUT THE WORLD WILL BE
A LITTLE BETTER BECAUSE
YOU WERE IMPORTANT
IN THE LIFE OF A CHILD.

—Anonymous

Appendix B

100 Ways to Praise and Encourage a Child

Wow! • Way To Go • Super • You're Special • Outstanding • Excellent • Great • Good • Neat • Well Done • Remarkable • I Knew You Could Do It • I'm Proud Of You • Fantastic • Super Star • Nice Work • Looking Good • You're On Top Of It • Beautiful • Now You're Flying • You're Catching On • Now You've Got It • You're Incredible • Bravo • You're Fantastic • Hurray For You • You're On Target • You're On Your Way • How Nice • You're Smart • Good Job • That's Incredible • Hot Dog • Dynamite • You're Beautiful • You're Unique • Nothing Can Stop You Now • Much Better • Good For You • I Like You • I Like What You Do • I'm Impressed • You Are Clever • You're A Winner • Remarkable Job • Beautiful Work • Spectacular • You're Precious • You're Darling • You're Terrific • Atta Boy • Atta Girl • Congratulations • You've Discovered The Secret • You Figured It Out • Hip, Hip, Hurray! • I Appreciate Your Help • You're Getting Better • Yeah! • Magnificent • Marvelous • Terrific • You're Important • Phenomenal • You're Sensational • Super Work • You're Very Creative • You're A Real Trooper • You Are Fun • You Did Good • What An Imagination • I Like the Way You Listen • I Like How You're Growing • I Enjoy You • You Tried Hard • You Care • You Are So Thoughtful • Beautiful Sharing • Outstanding Performance • You're A Good Friend • I Trust You • You're Important • You Mean A Lot To Me • That's Correct • You're A Joy • You're A Treasure • You're Wonderful • Awesome • A+ Job • You Did Your Best • You're A-Okay My Buddy • You Made My Day • I'm Glad You're My Kid • Thanks For Being You • I Love You!

Also: A Pat On The Back • A Big Hug • A Kiss • A Thumbs Up Sign • A Warm Smile

Adapted from material from Charter Hospital, Tucson, Arizona

Appendix C

Leadership Styles

	Autocratic Style	Democratic Style	Permissive Style
Characteristics of Parents:	• Keep (over-use) power. • Impose their will thru rigid rules. • Little flexibility, freedom. • Use force, pressure and punishment. • Demand "respect" (fear). • Make all decisions/rules; demand compliance. • Only one right way. • Feelings ignored.	• Share power. • Lead with kindness and firmness. • Treat others with respect; flexibility. • Treat kids as responsible, worthwhile people. • Encourage kids to make decisions, think for themselves. • Let kids be who they are, do things their way.	• Abdicate power. • No rules, structure; chaos results. • Too much freedom. • Believe they have no rights. • Absent (physically or emotionally), or are simply not interested.
Feelings of Parents:	• Superior (one-up) and "in control". • Untrusting of children. • Afraid of environment. • Lonely. Low self-esteem. • Burdened with responsibility.	• In charge, yet flexible. • Respect. Cooperative. • Trusting of self and kids. • Sensitive to others' feelings. • High self-esteem.	• Powerless, out of control. • Confused and angry. • Disrespected. • Low self-esteem.
Feelings of Children:	• Powerless, out of control. • Untrusting. Guilty. • Hostile and angry. • Dependent and submissive. • Afraid. Unsafe. • Low self-esteem.	• Worthwhile. Important. • Trusted and respected. • Self-confident, self-respecting. • Eager to cooperate. • Safe • High self-esteem.	• Powerless, out of control. • Unloved. • Confused, discouraged. • Dependent. Rejection. • Can't cope with routine. • Unsafe • Low self-esteem.
Characteristics of Children:	• Lack a sense of personal responsibility. • Self-rejecting & lonely. • Compliant or defiant. • Second-guessing common. • Always feel one-down, even when grown.	• Responsible. Respectful. • Self-disciplined. • Self-determining. • Understand cause-effect relationships. • Can be friends, equals with parents.	• Don't respect feelings of others. • Think they have a right to do exactly as they wish. • Little awareness of social reponsibility. • Have trouble with limits, yet hunger for them.

(See Chapter 11 for discussion.)

Appendix D

The Power of Expectations

Daddy expects me to be grown up.
If I prove to him that I am grown up,
he will love me.
But I feel frightened
because I am just a little kid.
And I feel terrified that he will
find out that I am frightened
and not grown up
and will not love me.
So I pretend not to be terrified
and he is proud of my being
what I am not.
Now he thinks that I am grown up
and I breathe a sigh of relief.
But now that I am who I am not,
he expects me to be even more of who
I am not which terrifies me all the more
because I am now expected to be more of
someone I never was.
To complicate matters, he says I should never lie.
So if I tell him that I am not grown up,
he will be proud of my telling him the truth.
But I can not tell the truth
about not telling the truth
because that is admitting to a lie.
Therefore, I must try harder
to be who I am not.

—Anonymous

Appendix E

Locus of Control

EXTERNAL	INTERNAL
Listen mostly to outside voices ("should," "have to").	Listen mostly to inner voices, intuition ("want to," "choose to").
Live life based on who they are supposed to be.	Live life based on who they are.
Avoid personal responsibility; then when something goes wrong, can blame others.	Accept responsibility for themselves, for their behaviors, and the consequences.
Trust others more. Look to others to take charge, to take care of them.	Trust themselves more, yet listen to others. Take charge of their own lives.
Have more confidence in others than in themselves.	Have increasing self-confidence.
Are vulnerable to pressure, manipulation, exploitation.	Think and make their own decisions; can resist external forces.
Give power away, then feel power-less.	Have a sense of personal power.
Feel helpless, out of control, like victims.	Feel in control of life; are pulling their own strings.
Worry about what their peers or neighbors think.	Care more about what they themselves think.
Have low self-esteem.	Have high self-esteem

(See Chapter 21 for discusion.)

Resources Available to Parents

Often during the years of parenting, I felt very isolated. I did not know how to make friends, or how to be a friend. (Talking only about husbands and kids as I'd learned to do is not a basis for friendship.) At that time, I also did not appreciate the importance of friendships, especially when relatives are distant. I was not aware that it was my responsibility to reach out, to find, to create supports. I now know that I am responsible for developing the self-support, people-support, and system-support that I need.

Though I felt isolated, I was, in fact, not alone. There were thousands of people around me, but I didn't have the self-confidence, assertiveness, or people-skills to ask for what I needed. My hope, in writing this book, is to teach you those skills and to encourage you to reach out to others—for friendship, for fun, for support. Don't be afraid to ask for help or support! *You are not alone.*

- Create your own group. With a few friends, you can fashion exactly what you want for yourself.
- Many churches and temples are family oriented. If yours is not, express your needs. Ask for the support you want. Your needs are not yours alone but are shared by others.
- Classes, workshops, counseling, and support are available for parents through community agencies, community colleges, and parenting centers.

If you have difficulty locating what you need, your county mental health center should have information on local resources. Remember, whatever you're looking for, you'll find.

If you feel overwhelmed at times, don't panic. Sometimes what you need is to get away from the kids for a while—walk in the woods, visit a friend, go dancing—to help you relax and regain perspective.

Take good care of yourself because I'm counting on you to take good care of your children.

175

Recommended Reading

Black, Claudia. *It Will Never Happen To Me.* (Denver, Col.: M.A.C. Publishers, 1982).

Briggs, Dorothy Corkille. *Your Child's Self-Esteem.* (New York: Doubleday, 1970).

Clarke, Jean Illsley. *Help! For Parents and Children* (a series of books covering developmental stages from birth to 19 years). (New York: Harper & Row, 1986).

Clarke, Jean Illsley. *Self-Esteem: A Family Affair.* (Minneapolis, Minn.: Winston Press, 1978).

Dinkmeyer, Donald, and Gary D. McKay. *The Parent's Handbook: Systematic Training For Effective Parenting.* (Circle Pines, Minn.: American Guidance Service, 1982).

Gil, Eliana. *Outgrowing the Pain.* (New York: Dell Publishers, 1983).

Green, Christopher. *Toddler Taming.* (New York: Ballantine Books, 1984).

Palmer, Patricia. *Liking Myself.* (San Luis Obispo, Calif.: Impact Publishers, 1977).

Palmer, Patricia. *The Mouse, the Monster, and Me.* (San Luis Obispo, Calif.: Impact Publishers, 1977).

Palmer, Patricia. *Teen Esteem.* (San Luis Obispo, Calif.: Impact Publishers, 1989).

Sher, Barbara. *Wishcraft: How to Get What You Really Want.* (New York: Viking, 1979).

Notes

Epigraph

1. Leo F. Buscaglia, Ph. D., *Living, Loving and Learning,* (Ballantine Books, 1983) p. 262. Used by permission of the author.

Chapter One

1. From the author's workshop brochure "Building Self-Esteem in Children".

Chapter Two

1. Henry David Thoreau, quoted in *2,715 One-Liner Quotations for Speakers, Writers and Raconteurs* by Edward F. Murphy (New York: Crown Publishers, 1981).
2. From a lecture by Foster Cline, adult and child psychiatrist, Evergreen, Colorado.

Chapter Three

1. Eleanor Roosevelt, *This is My Story, 1937.*
2. Affirmation from Jack Canfield tapes, *Self-Esteem: The Key to Success,* a six-cassette album available from Self-Esteem Seminars, 17156 Palisades Circle, Pacific Palisades, CA 90272.

Chapter Four

1. Eric Hoffer, quoted in *Bits and Pieces* (Fairfield, NJ.: Economics Press September 1986).
2. Samual Osherson, "Finding our fathers," Utne Reader, (April/May 1986).
3. Mildred Newman, Bernard Berkowitz with Jean Owen, *How to be Your Own Best Friend* (New York: Random House, 1973).
4. Leo F. Buscaglia, Ph. D., *Living, Loving and Learning* (N.J.: Slack, Inc. 1982). Used by permission.

Chapter Five

1. John Powell, *The Secret of Staying in Love* (Allen, Tex.: Argus Communications, 1974).
2. Julie Rigg and Julie Copeland, *Coming Out! Women's Voices, Women's Lives* (Melbourne N.S.W., Australia: Nelson Press, 1985).
3. Parent Effectiveness Training teaches listening skills based on Rogerian counseling principles.
4. Leo F. Buscaglia, Ph. D., *Loving Each Other* (Thorofare, N.J.: Slack, 1984).

Chapter Six

1. Virginia Mae Axline, *Dibs: In Search of Self* (Boston, Mass.: Houghton Mifflin, 1964).
2. Concepts adapted from Dr. Pat Palmer, *The Mouse, the Monster and Me* (San Luis Obispo, Calif.: Impact Publishers, 1977).
3. Ibid.
4. "Saying 'no' means..." and the value of "no"... exercise from Claudia Black.

Chapter Seven

1. Anne Morrow Lindbergh, quoted in Murphy, loc. cit.
2. Dorothy Corkille Briggs, *Building Self-Esteem in Children* (Garden City, N.Y.: Doubleday and Co., Dolphin Books, 1975).
3. Claudia Black, *It Will Never Happen To Me* (Denver, Col.: M.A.C. Publications, 1982).
4. T. Gordon, *Parent Effectiveness Training* (N.Y.: Wyden, 1973).
5. Concepts expanded from Briggs, loc. cit.
6. Henry David Thoreau, quoted in Murphy, loc. cit.
7. Concepts adapted from a Nathaniel Branden tape.
8. Leo F. Buscaglia, *Loving Each Other,* loc. cit.
9. Concept from Jack Canfield Self-Esteem tapes, loc. cit.
10. Lewis B. Smedes, *Forgive and Forget* (N.Y.: Pocket Books, Division of Simon and Schuster, 1984).
11. Clyde Reid, *Celebrate the Temporary* (N.Y.: Harper and Row Publishers, Inc., 1972).
12. Matthew Fox, *Meditations with Meister Eckhart* (Santa Fe: Bear and Co., 1983).
13. Chart excerpted from Gilda Gussin and Anne Burbaum, *Self-Discovery: Developing Skills* (Boston: Learning for Life Management Sciences for Health, Boston, 1984).

Chapter Eight

1. Matthew Fox, *Original Blessing* (Santa Fe: Bear and Co., 1983).

2. Concepts adapted from Jean Illsley Clarke, *Self-Esteem: A Family Affair* (Minneapolis, MN: Winston Press, 1978).
3. Ibid.
4. T. Gordon, loc. cit., p. 45.
5. Sidney Simon, from a presentation at the Calif. Self-Esteem Conference, Santa Clara, California, 1988.

Chapter Nine

1. From Robert Ricker, *Love Me When I'm Most Unlovable,* Reston,VA: National Association of Secondary School Principals.
2. Concepts adapted from Illsley Clarke, loc. cit.

Chapter Eleven

1. Marilyn French, *Beyond Power—On Women, Men, and Morals.* (New York: Ballantine Books, 1985).

Chapter Twelve

1. Kaleel Jamison, *The Nibble Theory and the Kernel of Power* (NY: Paulist Press, 1984).
2. Mary Fran Gilleran, I.H.M., "Blowing the Whistle on Oppression", Kindred Spirits Newsletter, Detroit, Michigan, Vol. 6, No. 3, Jan./Feb. 1988.
3. Kathleen Hallahan, "Why So Violent?", Foundation News, May/June 1986.
4. American Journal for Public Health, "Child Injury Deaths", Vol. 79, March, 1989.
5. Anthony V. Bouza, "The Epidemic of Family Violence", *Surgeon General's Workshop on Violence and Public Health Report* (Washington DC: Health Resources and Services Administration of U.S. Public Health Service, 1986).
6. Paula Gunn Allen, "Connecting With the Source", Creation, Vol. 2, No. 6, Jan./Feb. 1987.
7. To join Parent Action mail $5 to 230 N. Michigan, Suite 1625, Chicago, Illinois 60601.
8. Dr. T. Berry Brazelton, quoted in Chicago Tribune Tempo, Oct. 21, 1988.

Chapter Thirteen

1. From a cartoon by Ashleigh Brilliant, copyright 1982, Santa Barbara CA: Pot-Shots # 2369.
2. Concepts adapted from Donald Dinkmeyer and Gary D. McKay, *The Parents Handbook: Systematic Training for Effective Parenting* (Circle Pines, MN: American Guidance Service, 1982).

3. Bruno Bettelheim, "Punishment versus discipline", *The Atlantic,* v. 256 (November 1985), p. 52.
4. H.S. Glenn and B. J. Wagner, *Developing Capable People,* Instructor's manual. Privately printed. Undated.
5. Kenneth Blanchard and Spencer Johnson, *The One-Minute Manager* (N.Y.: Berkley Books, 1981).

Chapter Fourteen

1. Garrison Keeler, National Public Radio Program, July 2, 1989.
2. U.S.A. Today, September 11, 1986.
3. U.S.A. Today, January 21, 1985.

Chapter Fifteen

1. Jo Coudert, *Advice from a Failure* (N.Y.: Stein and Day Publishers, Briarcliff Manor, 1965).
2. Jesse Jackson, from a speech to the Denver Public Schools Push/Excel Program, August, 1979.

Chapter Sixteen

1. Statement made by author's son, Felix, at age 13.
2. Attributed to the late Virginia Satir.
3. J.W. Prescott, "Body pleasure and the origins of violence," *The Futurist,* April 1975, pp. 63-74.
4. Jules Older, Ph. D. "A restoring touch for abusing families." *The International Journal of Child Abuse and Neglect,* Vol. 5, No. 4 (1981). Exercise devised by occupational therapist, Franceska Banga.
5. Exercise adapted by Martha Belknap.
6. For information on P.R.E.S., contact Jeanne St. John, Ph.D., Director. Santa Cruz County Office of Education, 809 Bay Avenue, Suite H, Capitola, California 95010.
7. Quoted in William Shirer's *The Rise and Fall of the Third Reich (New York: Simon and Schuster, 1960).*
8. Linda Tschirhart Sanford, *The Silent Children* (Garden City, New York: Anchor Press/Doubleday, 1980).
9. Brandt F. Steele, quoted in St. Louis Post-Dispatch, August 8, 1982.
10. *A Course in Miracles* (Tiburon, CA: Foundation for Inner Peace, 1975).

Chapter Seventeen

1. Henry Ford quoted by Louis Tice in audiotape: "New Age Thinking for Achieving Your Potential" (Seattle, Washington: Pacific Institute).

Chapter Eighteen

1. Some concepts adapted from Matthew McKay, Martha Davis, Patrick Fanning, *The Art of Cognitive Stress Intervention* (Richmond, California: New Harbinger Publications, 1981).

Chapter Nineteen

1. David D. Burns, *Feeling Good: The New Mood Therapy* (New York: Morrow, 1980).
2. John Powell, loc. cit. p. 101.

Chapter Twenty

1. Gloria Steinem, "A new egalitarian life style," The New York Times, August 26, 1971.
2. Barry and Janae Weinhold, *Breaking Free of the Co-Dependency Trap* (N.H.: Stillpoint, 1989).
3. Jane Fonda, *New Workout and Weight-Loss Program* (N,Y.: Simon and Schuster, 1986).
4. Marilyn Ferguson, *The Aquarian Conspiracy: Personal and Social Transformation in the 80s* (Los Angeles: J. P. Tarcher, 1976).
5. Unpublished poem by the author.

Chapter Twenty-One

1. e. e. cummings, quoted in *The Magic-Maker,* by Charles Norman. (New York: Macmillan, 1958)
2. Attributed to psychologist Albert Ellis.
3. Bernie S. Siegel, M.D. *Love, Medicine, and Miracles* Copyright © 1986 by the author. Reprinted by permission of Harper and Row.
4. Siegel, loc. cit.
5. Ferguson. loc, cit.

Chapter Twenty-Two

1. Norman Cousins, *Anatomy of an Illness* (N.Y.: Norton, 1979).

Chapter Twenty-Three

1. Barbara Sher, *Wishcraft: How to Get What You Really Want,* (N.Y.: Viking Press, 1979).
2. Adapted from Sher, loc. cit.

Chapter Twenty-Four

1. Richard Bach, *Illusions* (N.Y.: Delacorte Press, 1977).
2. U.S. Current Population Reports, *Geographical Mobility,* March 83-March 84. Series P20 #407 (Washington, D.C.: U.S. Department of

Commerce Bureau of the Census).
3. *The Greeley* [Colo.] *Tribune,* January 11, 1978, and information from an interview with Bessie Cohea, 1982.

Chapter Twenty-five

1. Quotation on a patchwork quilt expanded by Denis Waitly.
2. Roly-poly, a.k.a. sow bug, or pill bug: any of various small, terrestrial crustaceans of the genus *Armadillidium* or related genera, having convex, segmented bodies capable of being curled into a ball.

Top   Side   Rolling

Postscript

1. Joanna Rogers Macy, *Despair and Personal Power in the Nuclear Age* (Philadelphia, Pennsylvania: New Society Publishers, 1983).
2. Matthew Fox, *The Coming of the Cosmic Christ,* (New York: Harper and Row, 1988).
3. Helen Caldicott, "Blessed Are the Peacemakers" calendar, (Berkeley, California: Golden Turtle Press, 1986).

Index

A

Alcoholic family systems, 135
Anger, 35-38
    analysis of, 35-36
    dealing with, 36-38
    expressing, ways of, 36-37
Asking skills, communicating, 25-27
Assertiveness, 25-28, 78
    asking skills, 25-27
    refusing skills, 27-28
Autocratic leadership style, 63-65, 68-69
    children's characteristics, 65
    children's feelings, 64-65
    parental characteristics, 64
    parental feelings, 64
Avoidance, 134

B

Behavior, and self-talk, 115
Beliefs, 109-112
    about children, 110
    components of, 110-111
    examination of, 112
Blaming
    criticizing response, 51-53, 55
    See also Criticism.
Body-image, 133
Bonding, 3, 8, 77

C

Child abuse, 101, 102-107
    crisis phone number, 106
    parental traits related to, 104-106
    types of, 102-103
Co-dependency, 127-128

Communicating

Communicating
    asking skills, 25-27
    assertive style, 25-28
    listening skills, 21-24
    love, methods for, 19-20
    monster style, 25
    mouse style, 25
    open-ended questions, use of, 26
    refusing skills, 27-28
    sending skills, 25-26
    words, power of, 43-49
Comparison, 137-139
Competition, danger of, 137-139
Conflicts, problem solving, 93-99
Criticism, 44-46, 48-49
    criticizing response, 51-53
    crooked communication, 44-45
    killer statements, 44
    versus feedback, 48
    "you" statements, 45
Crooked communication, criticism, 44-45

D

Democratic family, 86
Democratic leadership style, 67-69
    children's characteristics, 68
    children's feelings, 67-68
    parents characteristics, 67-68
    parents feelings, 67
Discipline, 79-87
    guidelines for, 87
    natural/logical consequences
        approach, 80, 81, 85
    and parental self-discipline, 85
    physical punishment, 85
    reactions to punishment, 83, 84
    and rescue behavior, 81, 82

reward/punishment system, 82-85
    use of term, 79, 80
Dissatisfaction, chronic, 40-41
Divorce, 74, 97, 158
Dualistic thinking, 136-137

E

Eating disorders, 65, 133
Empowerment, 71-78
    See also power.
Extended families, 157-160
    varieties of, 159-160

F

Faulty thinking, 115-118
    blaming, 117
    catastrophizing, 116-117
    having to be right, 117-118
    overgeneralization, 117
    personalization, 116
    polarized thinking, 116
    projection, 116
Feedback, self-esteem builders, 46-49
Feelings, 29-42
    acceptance of children's, 29-30
    anger, 35-38
    appropriate expression of, 30-31
    coping methods, 42
    forgiveness, 39-40
    gratitude, 40-41
    guilt, 33-35
    journal, use of, 31
    negative feelings, 30
    relationship to thoughts, 31
    repressing feelings, 31
    resentment, 38-39
    and self-talk, 115
    trust, 31-33
    See also specific feelings.
Forgiveness, 39-40
    process of, 39-40
    purpose of, 39

G

Gender definitions, 77-78
Generalized guilt, 34-35
Gifts/material possessions, negative
    effects, 19
Grandparents, 157-159
Gratitude, 40-41
    versus dissatisfaction, 41
    and tension, 41
Guidance, 89-92
    child's need for, 89
    and television viewing, 90-92
Guilt, 33-35
    generalized guilt, 34-35
    minimizing guilt, 35
    parental statements related to, 34-35
    specific guilt, 34-35

H

High self-esteem, sources of, 10
Honesty, value of, 32

I

Internalizing self-esteem, guidelines for,
    6,7
I-statements, negative behavior, 47

K

Killer statements, criticism, 44

L

Labels, and children, 43, 68, 112, 136-137
Leadership, 57-69
    autocratic leadership style, 63-65, 68-
        69
    components of, 57-58
    democratic leadership style, 63, 67-69
    and love, 63
    permissive leadership style, 63, 65-67
    proactive leadership, 58-59
    reactive leadership, 58-59
    and re-visioning the family, 59-61
    See also specific styles.
Listening skills, 21-24
    active listening, tasks involved, 22-23
    importance of, 21-22
    and problem solving, 94-95
    reflecting feelings, 22-23
Locus-of-control, 145-148
    of children, 145

external, 34, 84, 145-146
internal, 34, 60, 145-148
and self-esteem, 147
Love, 17-20
  communicating love effectively, 19-20
  and men, expression of, 17-18, 77
  negative expresions of, 18-19
  and parental leadership, 63
  positive expressions of, 19-20
  self-love, 8
  unconditional love, 6, 7
Low self-esteem, sources of, 9

M

Marshmallowing response, 51-53
Martyrdom, negative effect, 18
Mistakes
  children's, handling of, 124
  learning from, 123-124
Monster style, communicating, 25
Mouse style, communicating, 25

N

Native American, tradition, 59, 76-77
Natural/logical consequences approach,
  80-81, 85
Negative behavior
  dealing with, I-statements, 47
  and feedback, 47-48
  substitution method, 47
Negative influences, protection skills for,
  13-15
No, learning to say no, 27-28
Nurturing response, 51-53

O

Objectification
  dangers of, 139-142
Overpermissiveness, negative effect, 18
Overprotection, negative effect, 19

P

Parenting, giving and receiving, 2-3
Parenting responses, 51-55
  criticizing response, 51-53
  marshmallowing response, 51-53

methods for changing, 53-55
nurturing response, 51-53, 55
structuring response, 51-53, 55
Perfectionism, 32, 41, 121-125
  alternatives to, 123-125
  difficulties related to, 121-123
  and dissatisfaction, 41
  meaning of, 121
Permissive leadership style, 65-67
  children's characteristics, 66-67
  children's feelings, 66
  parental characteristics, 65-66
  parental feelings, 66
Physical punishment, 85, 103
Play, 149-153
  for adults, 150
  and immune system, 152-153
  and learning, 149-150
  parent/child play, 149, 151-153
Power
  associations, 72-73
  dimensions of, 74-75
  games, 73-74
  sharing with children, 69
Proactive leadership, 58-59
Problem solving, 93-99
  barriers to, 95-96
  guidelines for, 97-99
  listening and, 94-95
  win-lose approach, 96
Put-down, self, 114-115, 128-129

R

Reactive leadership, 58-59
Refusing skills, communicating, 27-28
Relationships
  always pleasing others, 131-132
  objectification, 139-142
  over-responsibility for others, 132
Rescue behavior, 81-82
Resentment, 38, 39
  price of, 39
Reward/punishment system, 82-85
  disadvantages of, 82-83, 85
  options to, 83-84

S

Self-care, exercise for, 130

Self-defeating behavior
  alcoholic family systems, 135
  avoidance, 134
  body-image and, 133
  comparison, 137-139
  dualistic thinking, 136-137
  faulty thinking, 115-118
  objectification, 139-142
  over-responsibility for others, 132
  pleasing others (always), 131-132
  self-sacrifice, 129-131
  self put-downs, 128-129
  separating person from behavior, 136-
    137
  sexism/racism, 139-140
  win-lose system, 142-143
Self-discipline, parental, 85
Self-esteem
  development in children, 5-10
  from external sources, 6
  high self-esteem sources of, 10
  increasing, exercise for, 11, 12
  internalizing, guidelines for, 6-7
  low self-esteem, sources of, 9
  and making mistakes, 124
  negative influences, protection skills
    for, 13-15
  and parental responses, 51-55
  and saying no, 27
  and self-love, 8
  and unconditional love, 6, 7
  words as builders of, 46-49
  See also specific topics.
Self-fulfilling prophesy, 137
Self-image
  and positive behavior, 115
  and self-talk, 113
Self put-downs, 128-129
Self sacrifice, 129-131
Self-talk, 113-119
  affirmations, 118-119
  and behavior, 115
  example of, 113, 114-118
  and feelings, 115
  and self-concept, 114
  turnabout statements, use of, 49
  and unconscious, 119
Sexism/racism, 139-140
Specific guilt, 34-35
Structuring response, 51-53

T

Television viewing, 90-92
  advertising, 91
  dangers of, 91-92
Thoughts
  and feelings, 31
  See also Faulty thinking, 115-118
Time, quality, 19
Touching, 101-107
  and child abuse, 101, 102-107
  improving, exercises for, 102
  lack of, dangers, 101
  sexual/nonsexual, 101
  touch disorders, 101
Trust, 31-33
  building in children, 33
  damage to, 32
  definition of, 32
  and honesty, 32

V

Violence, 75-76
  See also child abuse.
Vision, 57, 59-61

W

Win-lose system, 142-143
Winning Families
  characteristics of, 161-163, 166-167
  and peaceful world, 165-167
Words (power of), 43-49
  criticism, 44-46
  and self-esteem, 43
  self-esteem builders, 46-48

Y

"You" statements, criticism, 45

ADDITIONAL BOOKS, BOOKLETS, AND TAPES:

Quantity:

Book:
_____ *The Winning Family* $9.95

_____ *The Winning Family* **Guide**
for Parent Discussion Groups $2.00

Individual Tapes: $8.95
_____ Building Self-Esteem in Children
_____ Increasing Your Own Self-Esteem
(For Teachers, Administrators:)
_____ Building Self-Esteem in the Classroom

Excerpts from **The Winning Family** *are now available as booklets:*

_____The Best Gift: Self-Esteem
_____The Power of Words/Communication Skills
_____Communicating Love
_____Discipline Without Damage
_____Dealing With Feelings
_____Common Barriers to Self-Esteem
_____Creating A Winning Family   each $2.00
_____A complete set of seven for only $7.00

California residents add 6.25% sales tax.
Shipping and Handling: Add $2.50;
$1.50 for 1-3 individual tapes.
Booklet prices include shipping
and handling.

Bulk Quantity

25	50	100
$1.50	$1.25	$1.00

Name _____

Address _____

City   State   Zip

MAIL TO: **LifeSkills Press** • c/o Publishers Services,
P.O. Box 2510 • Novato, CA 94948

✍ NOTECARDS ✍
from THE WINNING FAMILY

If you liked The Winning Family, pass along a notecard to someone special to you, or order a reminder for yourself. Our notecard series has black & white illustrations from this book with quotes on the back. (Insides blank.)

Each card may be ordered in sets of 10 for $6.00.
The Complete Set of 15 cards is available for $8.00.

Tear out and mail this order form with check or money order to:

LifeSkills Press
c/o Publisher's Services
Box 2510 • Novato, CA 94948

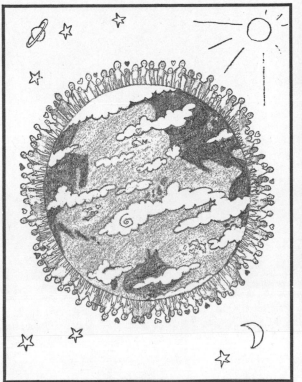

WF214

Quantity	Description	Amount
	Subtotal:	
	California residents please add 6.25%	
	Shipping/Handling add 10%	
	Send this Amount:	

Card orders may be combined with book/tape orders.

Ship to:
_____
_____
_____